The Raven and the Cross

Chippenham
Edington
Selwood Forest
Athelney
Egbert's Stone
Ellen
Edwina
Alfred
Guthrum
Sigfrid
Edmond
Cedric
Priest
Adam

THE RAVEN AND THE CROSS

John Tully

Illustrated by Derek Collard

British Broadcasting Corporation

The Raven and the Cross was created for the BBC-tv schools television Merry-go-Round programme (series editor, Claire Chovil) by John Tully, and will be shown for the first time early in 1974. The film was directed by Dorothea Brooking.

Published by the British Broadcasting Corporation,
35 Marylebone High Street, London W1M 4AA
ISBN 0 563 12472 5
First published 1974

Printed in England by Tonbridge Printers Ltd., Tonbridge, Kent

CONTENTS

The Raven and its Prey	Page 6
Lord, Deliver Us!	14
Lady of the Manor	22
A Dagger in the Church	29
Journey to the West	39
The Song of Cedric	48
King's Messenger	57
A Game of Chess	65
A Place and a Date	73
The Secret Army	83
The Whispering Air	94
At Egbert's Stone	103
Race to Battle	112
Clash of Arms	120
Let Wars Between us Cease	128
Fact and Fiction	134

THE RAVEN AND ITS PREY

To Wessex came the Viking bands
By paths that no one trod.
The Raven on their Banner stands,
The emblem of their god.

THE TALL trees of the forest muffled the sound of horses' hooves and the slow tramp of marching feet. The Viking army moved along the hidden path like a company of ghosts, silent and unseen, and their Raven Banner hung limply in the still, frosty air.

Guthrum rode at the head of his army with a group of senior officers, his jarls. Guthrum had a look of the Raven himself. His straight black hair fell to his shoulders and a black cloak was wrapped around him. His face was pale, his eyes cold and calculating.

A faint sound of another horseman was heard, coming down the path toward them. Guthrum drew up his horse and raised a hand to halt the men behind him. A single rider cantered into view. He was a big man with a large round face that split into a grin as he pulled up in front of his chief. His booming voice broke the silence.

"The Manor of Chippenham lies just beyond the forest, over the hill, an hour's ride away. There's no sign of a Saxon army."

Guthrum nodded. "I told you there would be no Saxon army. They were worn out by last year's battles. They'll be in their homes, around their firesides. They don't expect an attack in the middle of winter." He allowed himself a thin smile. "That is why we are here."

The big man threw his head back and laughed. "The gods gave you more cunning than a fox. We shall take the whole of Wessex by surprise." He pulled his horse around. "Let us not waste time in talk."

"Sigfrid!" called Guthrum sharply, and the big man paused. "Is there any sign that Alfred is at Chippenham?"

Sigfrid shood his head. "I think not. The manor looks almost deserted."

"A pity," said Guthrum softly. "I hoped we might have taken the king himself by surprise. But no matter. His turn will come."

He waved his arm to beckon the jarls. "Forward! We march on Chippenham at once."

The Manor of Chippenham lay in the valley of the River Avon. Its fields were neatly cultivated in narrow strips and in the midst of them lay the village, a huddle of timber cottages with thatched roofs. Overlooking the village, on a slight rise, was the big manor hall with its church and other buildings surrounded by a tall wooden stockade, and a deep ditch to serve as defence against enemies. Few people were out of doors on that hard winter's morning early in January 878.

Within the hall a servant lad was heaping fresh logs on a huge fire which burned on the hearth in the middle of the room. Smoke curled toward the opening in the roof above. Two big hunting dogs were stretched out beside the hearth, asleep, and a goat was quietly munching some of the straw which covered the floor.

A young girl stood in front of a big weaving frame, thrusting a shuttle between stretched threads, to and fro, back and forth. With each movement she became more impatient. At last she jammed the shuttle between the threads.

"I can't do any more of this," she said angrily, "I hate it!"

A little woman sat nearby spinning wool. She was hardly any taller than the girl and her face was lined with age. "Edwina!" she cried. "How many times have I told you? All young ladies learn to weave."

She stopped as the goat thrust its head under her arm, about to take a mouthful of wool. She slapped it sharply on the nose and the goat moved back a couple of steps.

Edwina turned to the little woman. "Ellen, please – why can't I go out hunting?"

Ellen sighed. She grew weary of the same old arguments. "You know very well your father does not wish you to go hunting. Hunting is for boys, not for young ladies!"

Edwina answered with a snort that was not at all ladylike. She pushed her hands out toward the blaze. Ellen's eyes turned toward the hearth and she gasped with dismay. She hurried forward, shoving the servant lad aside.

"Mercy, boy, what are you doing? Look there!" She pointed at two small sticks which lay at the side of the fire, one on top of the other. "Those are ash twigs, crossed! Don't you know that is a bad sign – an evil omen?"

The lad merely shrugged, but Ellen bent and uncrossed the twigs. "Some disaster will befall us," she muttered darkly, "I know it in my bones."

She looked up again, just in time to see Edwina making for the big double doors at the end of the hall.

"Edwina! Where are you going?"

Edwina stopped. Through one of the doors which was half open she could see sunlight sparkling on the frosty courtyard and she longed to be out in it.

"Let me go out riding," she begged.

Before Ellen could reply the door was pushed further open and a tall man came in from the courtyard. Though he was wrapped in a thick woollen housecloak he was shivering.

Edwina turned and bobbed politely. "Good morning, father," she said. Inwardly her heart sank. Now she couldn't hope to escape for a brisk ride over the hills.

"Good morning, child," said Athelwald, rubbing his hands. "I'm glad you're here. I want to talk to you. Shut that door first, I beg you." Edwina closed the door. Athelwald moved eagerly toward the flames leaping from the hearth. "My, but it's cold today. A hot drink, boy. Quickly, before my stomach freezes."

The servant hurried away. Ellen sank into a curtsy, but Athelwald was not looking at her. He pointed a stern finger. "What is that animal doing in here?"

Ellen looked at the goat as if she had only just set eyes on it. "Oh, mercy," she cried. "If I had known it was here I would have had it out in an instant!"

She grabbed the goat by the nearest horn and pushed it out into the courtyard.

Athelwald muttered as he warmed his hands. "It is not proper that a goat should be allowed to wander about the hall of a royal manor. The king may not be here in person, but that makes no difference. As his royal bailiff *I* am entitled to some respect!"

Ellen slammed the door shut and cast her eyes up. All this fuss about nothing! Dogs and hunting hawks were always to be seen about a manor hall. Why worry about a goat, or a few hens for that matter? It was just like Athelwald to fuss about little things. He had fussed for the past ten years, ever since he became bailiff. His job was to see that the manor ran smoothly when the king was absent, which meant that Athelwald was in charge most of the time. The king only visited each of his royal manors for a few weeks each year, to show his presence to the people, hear their complaints and settle their disputes.

"What do you want to talk to me about?" asked Edwina. Her father did not usually have much to say to her. Ever since her mother's death when Edwina was a small child, Athelwald had left her upbringing to her nurse, Ellen.

His face grew more cheerful. "Ah, yes! I have good news. I have arranged a marriage for you."

He beamed at her. Edwina stared at him in astonishment, not sure if she had heard him aright.

Ellen was the first to recover. She looked shocked. "Marriage? For Edwina? But she is only a child—!"

Athelwald waved a hand impatiently. "She is twelve years old. I have agreed on a contract for the marriage. The actual ceremony can wait a while."

Edwina heard her own voice speaking faintly, as if it came from someone else. "Who? Who am I to marry?"

"The Thane of Mildenhall," he replied with a note of triumph. "That is why I have been at Mildenhall these past three days. I would have spoken to you last night, when I returned, but as you had retired to your room I did not wish to disturb you." He rubbed his hands together in pleasure. "Isn't it a splendid idea? His lands will be joined with ours. We shall all be rich!"

Edwina stared at him in disbelief but he seemed not to notice.

"You will go to Mildenhall very soon and be presented to the Thane. Mind you take good care to please him!"

"No!" Edwina found her voice at last. "He's old and stupid! Do you know what people call him? The Goose of Mildenhall!"

It was Athelwald's turn to look astonished. "Edwina!" he gasped.

"I won't marry him!"

Athelwald threw back his head and pointed a finger at her. "You will do as you're told."

"I won't," she screamed, "I won't!"

She turned and ran to the doors, dragged one open and

disappeared into the courtyard.

"How dare she!" Athelwald was shaking with rage. "How dare she defy her own father!"

"I don't blame her!" said Ellen. She looked as angry as he did, like a little robin with ruffled feathers. "How can you sell your own daughter for land? The only child you have! If her mother were alive – God rest her soul – what would she think?"

Athelwald turned his fury on to Ellen. "Silence, woman! Remember your position. You are a servant in this house. As Edwina's nurse it is your duty to make her see sense. If you wish to live under this roof much longer you will teach her to obey her father with a willing heart!"

Ellen took a deep breath. She tossed her head and strode out of the hall. Athelwald's hands were trembling as he raised them in front of the fire.

The stone church with its squat, square tower, stood opposite the manor hall, across the courtyard.

Edwina was kneeling in front of the altar. Her eyes were raised toward a wooden cross that hung on the wall. Carved on it was a figure of Christ. With few friends of her own age to talk to, Edwina often shared her troubles with Him.

"You can't let it happen," she told Him firmly. "You can't let father marry me to that wretched old man. We agreed, didn't we, that one day I shall marry a handsome young thane, someone I can love with all my heart. You promised me! Oh, please make father change his mind!"

She heard a step behind her and looked over her shoulder. It was Ellen. Edwina rose and threw herself into the old woman's arms, sobbing.

Ellen was taken aback. It was not often that Edwina was moved to tears. She patted her. "There now, child. No tears. You're not one to cry. You're such a brave girl."

Edwina's sobs were as much in anger as in sorrow. "The Goose of Mildenhall!" she said bitterly.

"I know, love, I know." Ellen felt tears coming to her own eyes. "But what can we do? A daughter is her father's property, you know that as well as I do. Your father has a right to marry you to any man he chooses. At least you'll be sure of a good position as lady of a fine manor."

Edwina was not to be comforted. She drew back from Ellen, wiping her tears as if ashamed of them. "It's not fair! I won't be a piece of property, like a field or a horse. Men can marry or not as they want. Why shouldn't I?"

Ellen looked shocked again. "Mercy, child! A girl must do as she is told—" She stopped as Edwina strode up the aisle toward the door. "Where are you going?"

"I'm going out riding. I shall ride as far away from here as I can. Don't be surprised if I never come back!"

With that she was gone.

LORD DELIVER US

Softly under winter's cloak
Did Guthrum ride that day,
To fall upon the Saxon folk
Like Raven on its prey.

EDWINA hurried to the long, low building where the women had their quarters. As the bailiff's daughter she had a private space at one end, cut off from the rest by a curtain. She took a woollen cloak from its peg on the wall and fastened it round her shoulders with a plain silver brooch. She put on her riding boots. Then she set off for the stable, a large barnlike building close to the stockade.

It was dark in the stable. Big oak beams hung low overhead. These were covered with planks on top to form a second floor, used for storing grain and hay. A groom was washing down one of the horses.

"Saddle my pony – quickly!"

The groom hurried to a row of saddles and harness which hung on the wall at one end of the stable. Edwina waited impatiently, afraid that Ellen might warn her father and he would stop her going.

But Athelwald did not appear. Edwina led the white pony out into the sunlight. She hitched her long dress up underneath the cloak and sprang easily into the saddle. The men at the gateway nodded to her as she passed them, then the pony's hooves thudded on the light wooden bridge over the ditch beyond the stockade.

There were few people about as she cantered through the village and down the narrow track between the fields. Where these ended the ground began to rise, but the little pony was strong and took the hill easily.

Edwina gulped in the frosty air and her spirits began to rise in spite of her troubles. Of course she would not marry the Thane of Mildenhall. Jesus agreed she should not, so that was settled.

She was heading north. She knew that her boast to ride as far as possible was a foolish one. If she rode north very far she would leave Wessex altogether. She would find herself in Mercia, the great Midland kingdom which had been captured by the Norsemen. Two of their powerful chiefs had divided Mercia between them. A third chief, Guthrum, was still without a kingdom of his own. He was spending the winter with his army at Gloucester. When the warm weather returned he might be a threat to Wessex, but that danger was far away in the future. Or so Edwina thought. . . .

She cantered over the crown of the hill and there, in front of her eyes, was the Raven Banner. Under it rode a troop of horsemen. Beyond them, from the forest, came company after company of foot-soldiers.

Edwina reined her pony to a halt with a shriek of dismay. For several moments she stared at the Vikings, unable to believe her eyes. Then a large man with a red face, close to the banner, pointed toward her and urged his horse forward.

Edwina stared no longer. With another shriek she turned the pony's head and galloped back the way she had come.

She plunged down the hillside at breakneck speed and shouted to the few men in the fields. "Norsemen! The Vikings are here! Beware! Beware!"

Their mouths dropped open. At first they stared back at her in disbelief. Then they looked toward the northern hill and saw the Raven appearing at the top. Their faces grew pale and they turned to run.

"Vikings! Vikings! Beware!" yelled Edwina as she galloped through the village.

Women screamed and clutched their children. Men shouted to one another in helpless fear. They all ran toward the stockade.

Edwina was over the ditch and through the gateway ahead of them. She yelled at the guards who stood idly flapping their arms to keep out the cold. "The Norsemen are here! Let in the villagers and close the gate. Prepare to fight. Quickly – quickly—"

Shouts echoed among the buildings. Men called in terror to one another, and fumbled for weapons that were not ready. The first of the village people appeared, running to find safety within the gate.

Athelwald was sitting in front of the fire in the hall, sipping hot spiced wine from a large cup. He heard the shouts and rose to his feet, wondering what it was all about. Edwina burst into the hall.

"Father – the Vikings are here. A whole army – on the hill!"

The cup fell from his hand. Athelwald stared at her. "It cannot be! Not now – not in the middle of winter—"

"It's true, father! Get your sword quickly. I've ordered the men to close the gate as soon as the village folk are inside."

"Close the gate?" Athelwald shook his head fearfully. "No! We have no army to defend the manor. If the gate is closed they will break it down and murder us all."

He gathered his long house-cloak around him and made for the door. Edwina stepped into his path. Her eyes were blazing.

"But, father, you cannot surrender to Vikings! You must defend the manor, in the name of the king!"

"If the king himself were here, he could not defend the manor! We must surrender, and beg them for mercy. Get out of my way!"

He pushed Edwina aside and ran out to the courtyard which was filling with people from the village. Women sank to their knees and wailed to heaven, "Good Lord, deliver us! Deliver us from the fury of the Vikings!"

Athelwald thrust his way through the crowd to the gateway. Men were already dragging the big timber gate across the opening in the stockade, while others were fetching the heavy bars that would hold it in place.

"Open the gate," shouted Athelwald. "Leave it open, I say!"

The men paused, uncertain, then they pushed the gate back again alongside the fence. Fresh screams arose from the women.

The Viking soldiers were forming a short line on the brow of the hill, rank behind rank. Sigfrid stirred impatiently on his horse, eager for the action to begin. Guthrum waited more calmly. He cast his eyes over the sheltered valley and the low hills beyond.

"Good country for cattle-breeding," he observed.

Sigfrid snorted. "Better for hunting Christians!"

Guthrum eyed his second-in-command sadly. Sigfrid, like so many Norsemen, had little interest in farming. They had grown used to stealing their food from others rather than growing it themselves, and supposed they would go on doing so for ever. But Guthrum knew that was impossible. Somehow he would have to make them understand. . . .

He glanced along the lines of men on either side of him and decided they were ready. He raised his hand in a signal. A horn blew, and the charge began.

Guthrum and his jarls took the lead, holding their horses to a steady trot. The foot-soldiers followed at a run, screaming war-cries as they plunged down the slope. They trampled across the fields and into the village. Soon smoke began to rise from a burning house.

Guthrum led the riders over the wooden bridge and into the open gate of the stockade. The first foot-soldiers followed closely.

The villagers, waiting on their knees in a gesture of surrender, were forced to scatter. Swords and axes rose and fell like scythes, cutting down any Saxon within reach.

Edwina crouched under the eaves of the manor hall, unable to take her eyes from the frightful scene. The Viking soldiers passed her by, careless even in their killing. If a man stood within reach of a sword or a spear he might be struck down. If not, then he was fortunate.

She wondered what had become of her father. He was not in the courtyard. Suddenly, as if not fearing if she lived or died, she strode toward the church. A horseman plunged by her but his sword was raised on the other side. A soldier thrust his spear toward her but it only tore her cloak. She reached the door of the church unharmed and went inside.

The church seemed to be full of soldiers. They were hauling down the tapestries from the walls and grabbing everything of value they could see. One held the golden cross set with precious jewels that had stood on the altar. Others clutched silver candlesticks and bowls.

Then she saw her father. He was kneeling in front of the altar facing half a dozen Norsemen who were jeering at him. One of them was fingering the richly decorated cloak Athelwald wore. Another had a sword pointed at his throat. Athelwald had his arms raised to them pleadingly.

"I surrender the manor," he called out. "Have mercy upon me!"

He was answered by a roar of laughter, and the sword lunged forward. Edwina screamed, but the sound of her voice was lost among the shouts of the men. They moved away, taking the cloak with them. Edwina ran down the aisle and threw herself on her knees beside her father. She raised his head into her lap and blood poured over her dress.

A loud voice boomed from the courtyard. "Hold! The manor is ours! No more killing! No more looting!"

The cry was repeated. The soldiers in the church relaxed. One by one they went out to the courtyard, taking their plunder with them. The clamour died down.

Edwina was left alone beside the altar, clutching the dead body of her father.

LADY
OF THE MANOR

East and west the Raven soars
And who shall stay its flight?
Too late to raise the Saxon swords,
Too late to stand and fight.

Before the flames the people fly
And curse that evil day.
No time to mourn for those who die
No time to kneel and pray.

Town by town the country falls
Beneath the Raven's wing.
The Saxons, forced upon their knees,
Cry "Guthrum is our king".

THE SAXONS were allowed to bury their dead. Father Benedict the priest, had been slain while trying to prevent the soldiers from looting his church. Edwina herself said prayers for her father.

In the manor hall Sigfrid tore down King Alfred's banner, the Dragon of Wessex. He threw it to the soldiers in the courtyard, shouting, "Do any of you feel cold? Here's a blanket to keep you warm!" The dragon was torn to shreds.

Guthrum sat himself in the high chair and declared that Chippenham would be his headquarters in Wessex. The main body of his army began to set up camp outside the stockade and all the food in the village was taken to feed them.

Later that afternoon the Saxons were ordered to gather in the courtyard. They came, fearful that they would be slaughtered by the soldiers who stood guard around them. There was a murmur among them as Edwina appeared, very pale, with Ellen at her side. Men bowed as she approached, and women curtsied. A frail man with long white hair stepped forward. He was Bernard, the clerk who kept the records of the manor.

"Plead with Guthrum to spare our lives," he begged her.

Edwina was taken aback. "But how can I—?"

"Your father is dead, God rest his soul," said Bernard. "You are Lady of the Manor now."

Edwina realised with dismay that they were all looking to her as their leader. A mere girl she might be, but as the only child of a nobleman she must succeed him. It was God's will. She felt an urge to turn and run away, but she knew she could not. All her life she had enjoyed the comforts and privileges that came to her by birth. Now she must pay the price. These were her people and she must not fail them. Feeling absurdly small, she took her place in front of them.

They did not have long to wait. The doors of the hall were thrown open and the standard-bearer came out holding the Raven Banner. Then Guthrum appeared with several of his jarls. Many of the villagers, uncertain what to do, bowed again, but Edwina remained upright.

Guthrum's eyes flickered over them, then his thin, even tones broke the frightened silence.

"Who was in charge of this manor?"

Edwina stepped forward. Her voice rang out clearly. "My father was the king's bailiff. Your men have murdered him."

The jarls glanced at one another, not liking the boldness of her tone. Guthrum turned his piercing eyes on her. Then Ellen stepped forward. Edwina could see out of the corner of her eye that the old woman was trembling.

"'Tis my lady Edwina, daughter of Athelwald," said Ellen.

Guthrum nodded slowly. "I see. Very well." Then, as if the child were of no account he raised his head, addressing the crowd behind her. "Hear me, all of you. Your lives will be spared on one condition. You will acknowledge me, Guthrum, as King of Wessex in place of Alfred!"

The Saxons gasped in spite of their fear and whispered among themselves.

"You? A Norseman? King of Wessex?" It was Edwina who spoke aloud, with such contempt in her voice that the jarls murmured angrily.

But Guthrum ignored her. "In future you will owe your allegiance to me and to my banner." He pointed to the standard behind him. "The Raven, Bird of Odin, highest of our gods."

There was another gasp. That the Vikings should demand

their goods and even their lives the villagers understood. But how could Christians be loyal to a pagan god?

"No!" Edwina's voice rang out again sharply and everyone looked at her. She felt Ellen's hand on her arm, trying to warn her, but she shook it off. "You can't be King of Wessex. You're not even a Christian. All you know about is killing and stealing."

Several of the jarls moved forward, Sigfrid among them. Edwina waited to be struck down, and the crowd behind her pressed back, as far away from her as possible. But Guthrum raised his hand and the jarls halted. His voice was still calm, almost gentle. "That may have been so in the past—"

Edwina interrupted him. Words tumbled from her lips. "Three times King Alfred has paid you cartloads of silver to go away from Wessex!" This was true, as they all knew. Three times during Edwina's short life the Norse army had invaded Wessex and each time Alfred had paid them in silver and goods to go away again. "Only last year you made a treaty and swore your solemn oath you would never come back any more. Yet here you are again, looking for more plunder. Will it never end?"

To her surprise a thin smile appeared on Guthrum's lips as if he were amused by her defiance. "You do not understand, child. *I* am in command of this army now. I have not come here for silver." His voice rose suddenly. "I have come to take this kingdom and everything in it!"

Guthrum turned to face his jarls, as if he were trying to persuade them as well as the Saxons. "Even Norsemen cannot live by war and plunder for ever. Already our people have settled in other parts of this island. Northumbria is ours, and Mercia, ruled by our kings. Our soldiers have become farmers, raising their families on the land they have won." He looked at Sigfrid.

"Planting crops and breeding cattle!"

Guthrum swung round to the Saxons again. "But the greatest kingdom of them all is Wessex – and it shall be mine!"

In the silence that followed Sigfrid raised his sword and his heavy voice boomed out, "Kneel to Guthrum, King of Wessex!"

The Saxons fell upon their knees at once, bowing their heads. All except one. Edwina remained standing.

Guthrum turned his dark eyes on her. "You do not kneel?"

Edwina raised her chin. "I do not see the King of Wessex."

In one stride Sigfrid was in front of her. "Then your eyes shall be taught a lesson!" He raised his big hands to grasp her head, and his thumbs began to press into her eyelids.

Ellen gave a scream of anguish. Then Guthrum barked, "No!"

Sigfrid looked at his chief, puzzled.

"She is only a child," said Guthrum. "She will learn better. If these people are to be our loyal subjects, they must all be given time to learn."

Sigfrid lowered his hands slowly and turned away in disgust. Edwina felt faint and was glad of Ellen's hand supporting her arm.

To her relief Guthrum strode away, back into the hall, calling to his jarls as he went. "Tonight we shall feast. Tomorrow we shall march again, to conquer the rest of this land."

Since there was no army to oppose them, the Norsemen marched through Wessex in triumph, leaving a trail of people killed, houses burnt, churches and manors looted. Many of the Saxon thanes threw open their halls, offering surrender to save their lives. Others fled across the sea and took refuge among the Christian Franks. The common people had no choice but to submit to their new rulers.

Wherever the Norsemen appeared they proclaimed Guthrum King of Wessex and forced the people to kneel to him.

Edwina lived at Chippenham in a kind of waking nightmare. It did not seem possible that her father was dead and her home was the headquarters of an invading army. She and Ellen slept in the women's quarters as they had always done. Guthrum, impressed by Edwina's spirit, had given orders that she was to be left alone and she took advantage of this. She helped to run the manor much as her father used to do, not to make life easier for the Vikings, but so that she could arrange supplies of food for the servants and village people, many of whom were near to starving.

Almost every day there came reports of the Viking progress, and Edwina felt a growing sickness in her heart. At first she hoped that Alfred would somehow raise an army overnight. But there was no firm news of Alfred, only rumours. Some said he had fled to safety in France like so many of his thanes, but this Edwina refused to believe. Others whispered that he had been killed, and she prayed that this was not so.

At last Guthrum returned to Chippenham. His claim to be King of Wessex was no longer an idle boast. His companies were scattered about the country, keeping order in his name. At the same time they went on looting food, horses, weapons and anything of value they could find in the towns and countryside.

Edwina knelt by her bedside and called upon Jesus to help. "All these years Alfred has ruled Wessex in your name. You must save him now. You must save Wessex. You must save us all. . . ."

A DAGGER IN THE CHURCH

The Christian king must bear his Cross
And flee the Viking tide.
The king who has a kingdom lost
Must find a place to hide.

Most of the jarls returned to Chippenham with Guthrum after their campaign, to rest and celebrate their victory. They settled themselves in the manor hall, hanging their shields on the walls after their custom. The Raven Banner was again hung above the high chair.

Edwina kept to her corner of the women's house until Osric, one of Guthrum's senior officers, sent for her. She went unwillingly to the hall to find out what he wanted. The jarls were lounging on the benches and around the hearth. The hall reeked of their sweat and was noisy with their chatter.

Osric looked at Edwina down his long nose and spoke in clipped tones. "The king has orders for you. Since you are responsible for the servants here you will see that ample food is provided for the king and his officers, and that everything is done for their comfort. Do you understand?"

Edwina understood all too well. Guthrum expected her to act as his housekeeper. She was about to tell Osric that his friends could look after their own comforts when she heard voices close behind her. One jarl was saying to another, "We left the third company at Winchester. Two hundred men and twenty horses, and enough arms to keep the place under control. We'll have no trouble there."

Edwina bit back the sharp reply that was on the tip of her tongue. If she refused to run the household she would be banished from the hall, perhaps sent down to the village to live. But if she made some show of helping she would still have a free run of the manor. And the manor was Guthrum's headquarters, where he would receive reports from his army and make his plans for the future. . . .

Osric tapped his foot. "Well, girl, did you hear me?"

Edwina made up her mind. "Tell the king that everything will be done as he commands."

After that Edwina spent much of her time in the hall, apparently making sure that the servants did their jobs properly. She became so familiar a figure that the jarls took no notice of her and talked as if she were not there. One officer would speak of the ninth company, another of the seventh. Bit by bit Edwina learned where every company was stationed and what strength it possessed in men, horses and weapons.

One day she went down to the village, telling the guards that she wanted to arrange supplies of grain from the mill. In fact she went to see Bernard, the clerk.

"I want you to make a list for me," she told him.

Bernard shook his head sadly. "There is not much left in the manor to list," he said. "Very few cattle remain, and a few sheep—"

"Not that sort of list," said Edwina impatiently. "Have you a parchment and a quill? I will tell you what to write down."

Bernard searched out a sheet of parchment and his precious jar of ink. He sharpened a goose quill and Edwina began to dictate to him.

"First and eighth companies, guarding Chippenham. A total of 380 men. . . ."

Bernard wrote down all the information Edwina gave him. When the ink was dry she rolled up the parchment and hid it inside her dress.

"Now there is no danger of my forgetting the details," she said.

When she had returned to her quarters she hid the parchment in the bottom of her clothing chest.

Next day most of the jarls went out hunting, as they often did, but Guthrum remained in the hall. He sat in his high chair, silent and brooding. Sigfrid stayed with him, watching him anxiously. At last he filled a cup from a flagon of wine and offered it to Guthrum.

"Here, drink this," he said gruffly. "We all celebrate our victory except you. Take the wine and drink. Wessex is ours!"

Guthrum did not take the cup. He turned his dark eyes on to Sigfrid and asked, "Is it?"

"Of course it is!" said Sigfrid, puzzled by Guthrum's mood. "The Saxons are on their knees, hailing you as their king. What more do you want?"

Guthrum shook his head slowly. "They hail me with their voices, but not with their hearts."

He glanced toward the hearth and saw Edwina there, ordering a servant to bring more logs. The girl seemed to be there whenever he was in the hall. Was she really so anxious to serve him?

"Like that child over there," he said. "She serves us only because she is afraid of us. All these Christians are the same. They are taught to worship their king because he is chosen by their god. They don't worship me because they don't believe in our gods. While Alfred lives they still think he'll come back and set them free."

Edwina knelt and put a half-burnt log back on the fire. So Alfred *was* alive! She wanted to stand up and cheer.

Guthrum slammed his fist on the arm of the chair. "Why did we let him escape?"

Sigfrid snorted. "We couldn't stop him. He ran too fast."

Guthrum sighed and rose from his chair, but before he could reach the door it opened. An officer of the guard came in.

"We have a prisoner, Sire," he said. "Brought here from Dorchester. We believe he was one of Alfred's personal bodyguard."

"Bring him here," ordered Guthrum.

Edwina moved round the hearth, to keep out of sight as far as possible. Two soldiers brought the prisoner into the hall. His hands were tied behind his back, and his face was streaked with blood. They thrust him on to his knees in front of Guthrum.

"When did you last see Alfred?" asked Guthrum quietly. When he spoke quietly he was most menacing.

The man replied sullenly. "The king spent Christmas at Dorchester. He was still there when we heard of the invasion. He left the manor with most of his officers. A few of us stayed behind to organise resistance, but that was no use."

"Where is Alfred now?"

The prisoner did not answer. Guthrum clutched the front of the man's tunic, raising him to his feet and staring him closely in the face. "Has he gone to France?"

"No!" The man raised his head proudly. "He will not leave his kingdom. He will not let you take it from him."

Guthrum hissed, "Then where is he? Speak, or you die!"

Still the man held his head high. "The king has gone where you cannot reach him, beyond the forest of Selwood, into the marshes of Somerset. More than that I do not know. May God preserve him to save us all!"

Guthrum hurled the man backward into the arms of the soldiers. "Take him away!"

The soldiers dragged their prisoner out of the hall. Guthrum began to pace up and down while Sigfrid became restless.

"Let us after him at once," boomed Sigfrid. "Let us comb the marshes from end to end, till we find him!"

Guthrum's lip curled. "Comb the marshes? Why, it would take every man we have to search that area, and still he might escape us. Meantime the rest of the country could rise in rebellion." His fists clenched and his voice rose louder. "Let him hide in his marshes. Let him rot there!"

He grabbed the cup that Sigfrid had offered him and drank deeply from it. "We shall not try to find him. One day he will come back – and then we shall see who is king of Wessex!"

Edwina hurried from the hall, her heart pounding with excitement. At last she knew where Alfred could be found. Her mind began at once to work out a plan, some means by which she could escape from Chippenham. She went to the women's house.

And there was Osric, waiting for her. With two of his men he was making a search of the Saxon's quarters, looking for hidden weapons. The clothes from Edwina's chest were spilled on the floor and Osric was holding the parchment which she had hidden there. He thrust it under her nose. His finger pointed at an entry which read, "Eleventh company, in West Hampshire. 150 men, 10 horses."

"What is the meaning of this?" he demanded.

Edwina took a deep breath, and spoke as calmly as she could. "It is a list of supplies which I need. I cannot remember everything in my head." She pointed to the entry by his finger. "That says, eleven sacks of grain to feed 150 men for 10 days."

Then she held her breath. She had never yet heard of a Viking who could read, but Osric was very efficient. He frowned at the writing, aware that his men were watching him. Then he pushed the parchment into her hand.

"Yes, yes, I realise that. Just make sure that the supplies are obtained."

He stalked out and his men followed him. Edwina collapsed on her bed, clutching the parchment.

The church had been turned into a storehouse. Saddles and harness were hung round the walls. Spears, battle-axes, and daggers were held in racks, ready for use when needed. The carved figure of Christ on the cross still hung on the wall, though it had been knocked askew. Edwina knelt in front of it, her hands raised in prayer.

"Please see that Ellen does what I told her to do. Help me to make my plan work. And please hurry her up. I'm getting stiff kneeling here."

As if in answer to her prayer she heard Ellen's voice in the doorway. "Please spare a minute of your time, Sire. The child has been praying all morning. She can't sleep and won't eat. Truly, she is pining away and I fear for her."

Edwina bent her head lower and pretended to sob. She heard Guthrum answer impatiently, "What is the matter with her?"

"Before her father died he arranged that she should marry the Thane of Mildenhall. Now she is broken-hearted because the marriage cannot take place."

"The Thane of Mildenhall? He was one of the first to surrender to us. Does she want to marry *him*?" Guthrum sounded surprised.

"Oh, yes, Sire, since her father wished it. Please – let her go to Mildenhall to be married."

Edwina heard Guthrum's footsteps approaching her. She raised her face, hoping it would look tear-stained. He looked at her, a little curious.

"No use your praying here, child. This is not a church any more. Your golden cross has gone."

Edwina answered humbly. "Christian worship is a thing of the spirit. We don't need a cross to pray to."

"Indeed?" Guthrum seemed interested in this idea. He stepped past her to examine the figure on the wall. "Is this what you worship? A man put to death?"

Edwina rose to her feet. His back was turned to her. A terrible idea entered her head. It was no part of the plan she had worked out but she could not resist it. A rack of daggers lay nearby. She stretched out her hand and took one. Ellen drew in her breath in horror.

Guthrum was talking more to himself than to Edwina as he stared at the crucifix. "You should worship *our* gods. Gods of war and victory. Did you know that the quickest way for a Norseman to go to heaven is to die in battle?"

Edwina raised the dagger. Ellen opened her mouth to shriek but no sound came out.

"To die in battle. . . ." Guthrum mused. "And yet, we cannot go on dying in battles for ever. In future we shall die in our beds, or so I hope."

Edwina willed her arm to come down, to drive the dagger into his back. But the eyes of Jesus stared at her over Guthrum's shoulder, and she could not do it.

"Perhaps we need some other way to reach heaven," said Guthrum thoughtfully.

Edwina hid the dagger in her sleeve as he turned to face her. She spoke with true humility. "Please let me go away from here."

He walked past her. His thoughtful mood was over. He was a

king with work to do. "I've no men to spare for escorting you to Mildenhall."

Edwina nodded quickly to Ellen who was still trembling. Ellen realised what was expected of her. "Oh, Sire, there is no need for an escort. I will go with Edwina, if you will permit it."

Guthrum glanced at Edwina again. Her sudden humility was suspicious. Yet what harm could she possibly do?

He put a finger under her chin to raise it. "I don't trust you when you are humble. Perhaps you had better be gone from here. You may go to Mildenhall with your nurse. May your god protect you, for I cannot."

"I pray He will," said Edwina with feeling.

JOURNEY TO THE WEST

O who will win the victory
And who will bear the loss?
Which banner shall triumphant be,
The Raven or the Cross?

EDWINA was allowed to take her white pony since it was too small to be of use to the Vikings. She rode out of Chippenham soon after dawn with Ellen after her. Ellen was perched between two large saddlebags on a donkey aptly called Vixen. They took the road to the south-east, heading for Mildenhall. Edwina wanted to gallop as fast as she could go but Vixen would not move at more than an ambling walk.

Edwina stopped on the top of the hill, waiting for Ellen to catch up, and looked back at the manor with sadness. It looked so peaceful nestling in its valley in spite of the Viking tents around the stockade. She wondered if she would ever see it again.

Later that morning Chippenham lay far behind them and they were plodding slowly through a wood. Here Vixen decided that she needed a rest and stopped altogether. Ellen jerked on the reins in vain.

Edwina drew up the pony and looked round. There was no one in sight. She called over her shoulder, "I'm stopping here." She turned the pony off the path into the shelter of the trees.

"What for?" cried Ellen "Wait for me!"

She prodded Vixen with her heels and the donkey ambled forward again. She turned off the path to follow Edwina, and found her in a small clearing. The pony was tied to a tree. The saddlebag on the pony was open. Edwina had taken off her dress and was struggling into a heavy woollen tunic and a pair of trousers, the sort worn by peasant lads in the village.

"What are you doing?" gasped Ellen as she climbed off the donkey.

"I got these clothes from a shepherd boy," Edwina explained. "And I stole this from the church." She held up a dagger which glinted in the sunlight.

"Mercy, what for? You can't go to Mildenhall dressed like that."

"I'm not going to Mildenhall. I'm not going to marry that stupid old man, now or ever." She drew a leather belt around her tunic and stuffed the dagger into it. "I am going to find King Alfred."

Ellen's mouth gaped open and Edwina could not help smiling. "That was my plan from the start. I didn't tell you because – well, you might not have helped me if you'd known."

Ellen clutched Vixen for support. "I should think not indeed! Find Alfred! How can you—?"

"I know he is hiding in Somerset. Since I'm not a Viking but a loyal Saxon someone will help me to reach him."

Ellen spoke angrily. "But, child, you'll never get that far. You'll be torn apart by wolves – or else murdered by Guthrum's soldiers."

Edwina was pushing her hair up and covering it with a woollen cap. "There! Do I look like a boy? The Vikings won't bother themselves about a poor peasant lad, will they?"

With her rather plain features Edwina did look like a boy. She gathered up her dress and pushed it into the saddlebag where the parchment lay. "I must find the king, Ellen. I have information that will be useful to him."

Ellen waved her hands in the air helplessly. She had learnt long ago that it was no use arguing with Edwina.

"What will become of you?" she wailed. Another thought struck her. "What will become of *me*?"

"You must come with me, of course."

"No!" Ellen shook her head fiercely.

"But you must. This is your chance to serve the king."

Ellen raised her head. "Why should I serve him? I'm not a Norseman or a Saxon. I'm a Celt. My people owned this land before you Saxons came and took it from us. Now the Vikings are taking it from you. What does it matter to me which king I serve?'

Edwina turned in surprise. She had never heard Ellen speak like that before. She knew that the Celts were people who had lived in Britain since long, long ago, before the Saxons came and conquered the island piece by piece. Though the Celts were now mostly servants, they kept many of their old customs and beliefs. That was why Ellen was always so fearful of omens and goblins. But the Celts were also Christians, and Edwina reminded her of this.

"Alfred is a Christian king. That is why you must serve him."

Ellen sniffed, and Edwina lost patience with her. "Very well, go your own way. When Guthrum finds out I'm missing you can tell him what happened."

Ellen threw up her hands again. "Tell Guthrum? He'll say it is my fault. He'll have me put to death!"

Edwina climbed on the pony's back. "It's up to you. Which pack of wolves do you fear the most?" She dug her heels into the pony and moved away through the trees, heading south.

After she had gone some distance she stopped and listened anxiously. With relief she heard the sound of the donkey's hooves in the dry bracken and Ellen's plaintive voice, "Move, you wretched animal. Move, will you?"

Edwina smiled as Ellen appeared, but Ellen refused to smile back.

They travelled south for some distance before turning to the west, in order to keep well away from Chippenham. When night fell they knocked on the door of a farmhouse. At first the farmer

was reluctant to let in strangers, but when Edwina explained who they were and why they were travelling the farmer and his family welcomed them with all the hospitality they could afford.

Early next morning they set off again, heading for Somerset as fast as Vixen would allow. Soon after midday they ran into a party of Viking soldiers. Their leader pointed his sword at Edwina, demanding, "Who are you, boy? Where are you going?"

"My name is Edwin, sir," said Edwina, using the boy's version of her name. She pointed to Ellen. "This is my grandmother. My father was pressed into service by the wicked King Alfred. Now that Alfred has been defeated by your brave soldiers, my father is free again. We are going to join him. Please let us go, sir. We mean no harm."

The soldier looked at her ragged clothes and waved them on. Soon the Vikings were out of sight.

"I shall die of fear before this journey is over," said Ellen.

That night they reached a small village close to the forest of Selwood. The Vikings had been there first. The manor hall was burnt to the ground and so were many houses in the village. Several people were sheltering in the church, which had escaped burning, though all its valuables were gone. Edwina and Ellen joined them for the night.

They talked to the old priest who told them that the thane of the manor had fled to join Alfred.

"I would have gone with him had I been younger," said the priest.

"Do you know where the king can be found?" asked Edwina.

The old man shook his head. "He is hiding in the marshes beyond the forest. That is all we know."

The next morning he led them some way into the forest,

pointing out the path they should follow.

"Be sure to keep to the path," he warned them. "If you do not know this country it is easy to get lost in the forest. You may find no one who can help you on your way."

This was enough for Ellen. "I'll not die in the forest," she declared. "You can go on if you must, but I'm turning back."

She tried to pull Vixen round, but the donkey was munching grass and refused to obey.

Edwina pointed over Ellen's shoulder at the clear sky. "Look, Ellen – a shooting star!"

Ellen turned her head but saw nothing.

"Too late," said Edwina. "It's gone. It was over there, in the east."

Ellen's face had gone pale. "A shooting star! That is an omen of death!"

Edwina knew Ellen's opinion of shooting stars very well, but she answered innocently, "Is it really? In that case you mustn't go to the east. You had better come with me after all."

Ellen looked at the girl with suspicion. Then she mumbled to herself, "If the omens say so, I suppose I must."

They took their leave of the old priest and set off down the path.

The forest seemed to stretch to the end of the world. All that day and the next they travelled through it. Then sheets of water began to appear on either side of them, shallow lakes that spread even among the roots of the trees. They had reached the marshes. The soil became so soft that often the pony's hooves sank into it. Several times they had to get off and walk the animals through the worst patches, and the path kept changing direction. Edwina began to wonder if they were still on the path at all, but she did not say so to Ellen.

When it grew dark that night Edwina halted on the driest area she could find. At least the wood was dry enough to build a fire with it. She struck sparks from her flint and steel, and felt a little better when the flames took hold. They warmed themselves in front of it. Ellen took bread and cheese from the donkey's saddlebags and they ate in silence.

"I could eat more," said Edwina at last.

"I'm afraid you can't," said Ellen grimly. "There isn't any more. You ate too much yesterday. You look like a boy and you eat like one too."

Edwina looked in the bag. Their food was all gone. She had no spear to hunt with, or hook to fish with. She knew that if they did not soon find Alfred's camp they might starve to death.

"Perhaps we should move on at once," she said.

"In the night?" snapped Ellen. "That is madness. We shall stumble into a lake or be sucked into a bog. You had best get some sleep, child. I will keep watch." When spending the night in the open they took turns to stay awake.

"We'll find Alfred's camp tomorrow," said Edwina as bravely as she could.

"Shall we indeed?" asked Ellen doubtfully. "Which way shall we look?"

Edwina glanced helplessly around the circle of trees. Suddenly there seemed to be no path at all.

It was then they heard the distant baying. Edwina's sharper ears caught it first. She bit her lip, saying nothing, till Ellen raised her head, also listening.

"Do you hear that?" said Ellen. "It's wolves!"

Giving up any pretence at bravery Edwina threw herself into Ellen's arms. This time it was Ellen who found courage.

"Don't you fear," she said. "We'll keep the fire up and that'll hold them off. Maybe in the morning—"

Edwina clutched her tighter. "We're lost, Ellen. I know we are. We'll never find our way out of here!"

Ellen patted her and held her in her arms till Edwina fell asleep.

THE SONG OF CEDRIC

I sing my song
The whole day long
I sing for your delight.
I carol a tune
Beneath the moon
To speed the silent night.

EDWINA woke to hear a distant sound, rising and falling. She looked round quickly. It was day. The fire was a heap of embers. Ellen, who must have stayed awake most of the night, was now asleep.

Again she heard the sound, a little nearer. She listened for a moment, then she pushed Ellen to wake her.

"Eh? What is it? What is it?" cried Ellen. "Is it the wolves?"

"No," whispered Edwina, "it's not the wolves. It's a man, singing."

Ellen scrambled to her feet, straining her ears. Words reached them faintly through the trees.

"I carol a tune
Beneath the moon
To speed the silent night . . ."

Ellen drew in her breath. "Will he be a friend or an enemy?"

"We'd best keep out of the way until we're sure!" answered Edwina.

Quickly they unhitched the pony and the donkey, and led them out of sight among the trees. Then they waited.

A young man on horseback came into view. He was tall and slim with a short beard and long dark hair falling around his shoulders. His face was narrow and sensitive. The pony's reins hung loose. He was holding a lyre in one arm and was gently strumming it as he sang.

"You'll hear me call
Within the hall
Where torches brightly glow.
You'll hear me trill
Upon the hill . . ."

He stopped singing when he saw the remains of the fire. He slid off the horse, stirred the embers with his foot, and looked round nervously at the trees.

"Is anyone there?" he called.

Edwina strode forward. She took the dagger from her belt and raised it in front of her.

The young man drew back, obviously scared. "Are you a thief?" he asked. "I haven't any money. All I have is my lyre. You mustn't take that." He clutched it tightly.

"Who are you? What is your name?" asked Edwina, deepening her voice as much as she could.

"My name is Cedric. I'm a poet. I'm the best poet in the whole of Wessex." He said this as if it were a simple fact rather than a boast. He added, "Even the king thinks so."

Ellen came from the trees. "Which king do you serve? Guthrum or Alfred?"

Cedric hesitated. "The same one as you do."

"You mean Alfred?" asked Ellen.

He nodded with relief. "That's right, Alfred. I was with him at Dorchester during Christmas. When the Vikings came we all had to run away. I got separated from the others."

"Why?" asked Edwina.

"Because I ran faster than anyone else," said Cedric, and grinned.

Edwina looked at him sternly. "You're a coward!"

"Yes, I am," agreed Cedric. "I always have been. I can't help it. That's why I was singing just now. To keep my spirits up. It's lonely in the forest. I sing well, don't I?"

"Better than the wolves," muttered Ellen.

Edwina put the dagger back in her belt. "What are you doing here?"

"I stayed in hiding while the raids were going on. I waited till

things had settled down. Now I'm on my way to – er—" He paused, doubtful.

"To join the king?" asked Edwina eagerly. "Do you know where he is?"

"Yes – but—"

She let out a whoop of joy. "Then you can take us to him."

Cedric still looked doubtful. "I can, if – well, that is – no one must know where the king is hiding."

Edwina smiled at him. "It's all right. We're not Viking spies. In fact the king knows me well."

"He knows you? A peasant boy?"

Edwina laughed, took off her cap and let her hair fall.

"This is my lady Edwina, daughter of Athelwald, bailiff of Chippenham," said Ellen. "Alfred has met her many times during his visits to the manor."

"My father is dead and Guthrum has made his headquarters at Chippenham," explained Edwina. "We have escaped and we must find the king."

Cedric eyed her sourly. "A girl! You might have said so before!"

Cedric drew up his horse at the edge of a lake and pointed across the water. "There's the camp," he said.

The sun was setting behind the trees on the far side, and smoke from several fires curled lazily into a streaky-red sky.

"How did you know where to look?" asked Edwina.

"When I came out of hiding I met one of the king's messengers on the road. He knew who I was and he told me where I could find the king. I know this country well. I was born just the other side of the marshes."

He turned his horse along the edge of the lake.

It was growing dark when the sentries challenged them. Cedric was recognised at once.

"Ho, see who is here!" cried one. "The song-bird has come back to the nest."

There was laughter from the other guards but Cedric did not seem to mind. Though it was late there was a lot of activity in the camp. Men were chopping down trees and trimming off the branches to build crude shelters which they thatched with dried reeds. News of Cedric's arrival spread quickly. The men put down their axes and followed him to the main camp fire which stood in a large clearing.

"It's the poet," they shouted. "He's come to sing for us again."

It was as if his presence reminded them of a life they used to know, of feasts and songs in manor halls, in times of peace.

"Sing for us now!" cried a burly fellow, and the others took up the cry: "Sing for us, Cedric."

Cedric threw up his hands in mock dismay. He was really very pleased by their welcome. "Have mercy. I haven't eaten all day."

"Sing and you shall earn your supper," shouted the burly man, and the rest roared their agreement.

Cedric grinned. "Very well. Since you can't wait to hear me!" He climbed on to a pile of logs near the fire and took his lyre from the bag which hung round his waist. Silence fell among the men, their faces glowing in the firelight.

"I sing my song
The whole day long.
I sing for your delight.
I carol a tune
Beneath the moon
To speed the silent night . . . "

Edwina and Ellen were ignored. Edwina glanced across the clearing. One of the shelters, larger than the rest, stood under the trees and the light of a torch flickered inside. A man came to the doorway, attracted by the singing. He wore a red tunic and a heavy leather jerkin over it to keep out the cold. There was not much to distinguish him from the other men around the camp fire except that he was taller than most. His hair and beard were gingerish in colour. As he listened to Cedric the sternness of his face softened. Only his eyes remained sad, as if there was suffering in them, like the eyes of the carved figure on the cross at Chippenham.

Edwina moved quickly around the back of the crowd till she reached the hut. Then she knelt.

"May God protect you, Sire," she said.

Alfred looked down at her. He did not recognise her in her boy's clothing.

"My name is Edwina. I have come from Chippenham."

The king looked surprised, but put out a hand to raise her to her feet. His smile of welcome was enough to make all the hardships of the journey seem worth while, and Cedric's voice sounded more tuneful than ever.

"You'll hear me call
Within the hall
Where torches brightly glow.
You'll hear me trill
Upon the hill
And in the vale below.

I praise the king
And everything
On land or sea or sky.
So tell me true,
I beg of you,
Who . . . am . . . I?"

As the riddle-song ended a loud chorus of voices answered the question. "A song-bird! A nightingale! A sparrow!" they shouted. Cedric pointed to a man who called the right answer, "A thrush," and the rest cheered.

"This is valuable information you have brought," said Alfred. He was studying Edwina's parchment. He handed it to a tall, thin man in the garb of a priest. This was John, who was both the king's priest and his personal clerk.

Cedric, Edwina and Ellen were all eating heartily. Alfred had invited them to supper at his own table, inside the hut which he referred to dryly as his "manor hall".

"Perhaps there is more that you can tell me," said Alfred. "Guthrum calls himself King of Wessex now. What does he mean by that?"

Edwina pushed aside an empty platter. "He means what he says. He swears that he will not leave Wessex this time, however much you pay him. He wants a kingdom for himself, land where his men can settle down and make their homes. He says they cannot live by war and plunder for ever."

Alfred must have expected this answer for he nodded calmly. "They grow older and wiser, these Vikings."

Suddenly he lifted his head and his features twisted in a look of pain. Edwina quickly turned her head away. It was well known that the king suffered pains which came upon him without warning. No doctor had been able to rid him of them, and he did not like people to sympathise. The spasm passed as quickly as it had come, and he went on speaking as if there had been no pause.

"But it shall not be. The Raven must seek its nest elsewhere. Guthrum shall not have Wessex. If he won't be paid in silver he shall be paid in blood." A deep sadness came into his eyes, showing a different kind of pain, as he added, "It will weigh much more heavily."

The promise of battle roused Edwina. "When? When will you march from here to fight him?"

The king smiled at her eagerness. "When I have an army to fight with. It will take some time." Seeing her look of disappointment he went on gently, "Our soldiers are also farmers. They will not leave their fields to fight again until after Easter, when the seed has been sown."

Edwina was about to speak but Alfred continued, "And rightly so! What use is it to win a battle and save our country, if our people and our cattle die next winter for lack of food? The crops must be sown. Guthrum must wait till that is done, and so must I."

Edwina was not content with this. "But if you wait, people will think you have been beaten, that you are not going to fight at all. Then they will give in to Guthrum."

Alfred shook his head. "Oh, no, my child. Our men shall not grow idle while they wait. We shall fight a different kind of war. We'll give the Vikings no rest. Wherever they can be found in small numbers and whenever they least expect it, our men will appear and strike them down, and disappear again – like stinging bees!"

KING'S MESSENGER

O who will win the victory
And who will bear the loss?
Which banner shall triumphant be,
The Raven or the Cross?

SEVERAL of the men who had fled from their homes to join the king had brought their families with them. The women and children lived in a small group of huts in a separate clearing. Edwina and Ellen joined them. Though some of the women were the wives of thanes, they were all expected to help in running the camp. They cooked food at the fires and washed clothes at the edges of the lake. Edwina had always taken an interest in the smaller children in the village at Chippenham, seeing that they were properly clothed and fed. She had learnt how to play with them and keep them occupied. Someone was needed to look after the little ones, and Edwina soon found herself acting as a nurserymaid.

A few days after her arrival she had a dozen children sitting in a circle while she told them stories of their own country. Using a stick, she drew a rough picture of the island of Britain in the soft earth. Since she had very little idea of the actual shape it was very rough indeed. But she knew that Wessex was the most important kingdom and it lay in the south, all the way from Kent in the east to Cornwall in the west. She told them that their king, Alfred, had been the youngest of five brothers, so no one had ever expected that he would be king. Each of his elder brothers had died an early death and so, in 871, Alfred became King of Wessex when he was only twenty-two years old. That was seven years ago. He had tried hard to make good laws and give justice to everyone. And now everything was in ruins because of the hateful Vikings.

"Be not afraid, we shall win our country back!" declared Edwina. Her voice rose to high pitch. "We shall drive the Norsemen out of Wessex, and no one will ever take it from us again!" The children cheered.

"Bravo!" said a voice behind her. "You should lead them into battle. Guthrum would run at the sight of you."

Edwina turned. A lad, not much older than herself, was leaning against a tree, grinning broadly. He was good-looking, she noticed, but his clothes hung about him in tatters and his face was grubby. A mere peasant! How dare he mock her! She was, after all, Lady of the Manor of Chippenham. Unable to think of a cutting reply, she showed her contempt by ignoring him.

"You can all help to gather firewood," she said to the children.

They shouted and danced after her as she strode off with her nose in the air. She knew the boy was still laughing at her.

Later that day Edwina was told that the king wished to speak to her. She hurried to the hut and was admitted at once by the guards. A few thanes were seated on rough-hewn logs which served as benches. John, the priest, stood in front of a flat board, writing in his careful script on a sheet of parchment. Alfred was seated on a stool which served him as "high chair". He was holding the list of Viking companies which Edwina had brought.

Edwina curtsied before him and Alfred pointed to the list. "You say here there is a detachment of Guthrum's men at Wilton. There is also a note here to say that they were instructed to send supplies to Chippenham by the end of the month. Is that correct?"

Edwina nodded. "Yes, I heard Osric talking about it. I'm sure it is right."

"In that case we can expect supply wagons to move from Wilton to Chippenham in a few days from now?"

Edwina nodded again.

"Excellent! We must see they do not get there. Edmond! This is work for you."

A young lad in tattered clothes stepped forward from the shadows. It was the boy who had interrupted Edwina's lessons.

"This is Edmond, Thane of Woodbridge," said Alfred.

Edmond's eyes twinkled as he bowed to Edwina.

"Thane of Woodbridge?" she gasped.

Alfred answered grimly. "Edmond's father ran away from his manor and took refuge in France. I have therefore made it known that his title and his lands are taken from him. They pass to Edmond who refused to run away. He found his way here instead. Now he is one of my trusted messengers. He finds it useful to disguise himself as a peasant lad, just as you did." He turned to Edmond. "Edwina has lost her father too. He was killed by the Vikings."

Edmond's grin vanished and his face turned bright red. "Please forgive me," he said to Edwina. "I should not have mocked you."

Edwina's dislike of him melted away. "I forgive you. I'm sure you meant no harm."

Edmond turned to the king. "What do you want me to do?"

"Your manor lies north of Wilton. You will go back there and instruct your people in the method of secret attack. They must prevent the supplies reaching Chippenham."

"It shall be done!" said Edmond eagerly. He turned, making for the doorway.

"Take care, Edmond!" Alfred's voice halted him. "Remember that our object is to hurt our enemies as much as possible, at least cost to our own people. Do not take any foolish risks. That is my command."

Edmond bowed and went out to the clearing.

Edwina sighed. "I wish *I* could go and lead an ambush."

There were chuckles from the thanes. Alfred raised a hand to silence them. "You have spirit, child, but you must carry on with what you are doing here."

Edwina went back to her children, but in her heart she was not satisfied. She told herself that somehow she would find a better way to fight the Vikings.

Edmond saddled his horse. He gave a low whistle. A tall, sandy-coloured hound came loping from the trees, barking eagerly.

The day Edmond had left his home, when the Vikings were nearing Woodbridge, he had ridden for several miles before he discovered that his dog, Adam, was following him. The big hound, bred for hunting, had little trouble keeping up with the horse. Edmond had ordered the dog back again, but Adam had refused to go. Instead, he followed Edmond all the way to Alfred's camp, thus proving (so Edmond declared) that he was a loyal Saxon dog. Since then Adam had travelled with Edmond wherever he went on the king's business.

"Good boy, Adam," said Edmond. "We're going home again. We've important work to do."

It was a hard journey for rider, horse and dog. Edmond was very anxious to reach Woodbridge in time, so he travelled day and night with only brief snatches of rest and food. The journey was longer because Edmond took by-paths that would keep him out of the way of the Vikings.

It was barely dawn when he crossed the River Avon by the old bridge that gave the village its name. The villagers greeted him with joy. It was only a small manor, and the Vikings had not bothered to leave troops there. Within an hour Edmond had all the young men assembled in the hall.

They were excited at the prospect of action but puzzled by the idea of "secret attack". They had never heard of this kind of warfare before. Edmond told them what was happening in other parts of the country in response to the king's order. Viking soldiers wandering alone or in pairs were being set upon and killed, often during the night. Viking horses and food stocks were being raided, while the men guarding them were slain. Treasures looted from the manors were disappearing for a second time, to be buried under Saxon huts where the enemy could not find them.

Then Edmond explained his plan for attacking the supply train from Wilton. He encouraged the men to make suggestions of their own. Two of them volunteered to set out for Wilton at once, in order to bring back word when the wagons started out. By evening Edmond was satisfied that all was ready.

The heavy wagons lumbered slowly along a rutted road through a wood. They were piled high with sacks of grain and vegetables, and one was loaded with silver, pottery and other valuables. They were drawn not by horses or oxen but by Saxon prisoners, chained to the shafts. Each wagon had a Viking soldier in the driving seat, armed with a whip which he used to lash the prisoners forward. A small detachment of soldiers on horseback formed an escort.

In the midst of the wood the wagon train overtook an old peasant couple, a man and his wife, who were stumbling along the path. One of the soldiers shouted to them to get out of the way and they drew aside, clutching one another.

An arrow whistled from the trees and found its mark in the breast of the Viking soldier driving the foremost wagon. He slumped forward in his seat. The prisoners stopped pulling and the other wagons halted behind. The leader of the escort shouted a furious order. He was about to plunge off the path in the direction the arrow had come, but he never got that far.

Saxons rose on all sides, from behind bushes, dropping from the branches of the trees. Several more arrows flew into the pathway, aimed at the horsemen.

The "old peasant" and his "wife" threw off the cloaks they were wearing to reveal young men with daggers drawn. They leapt upon the wagons closest to them to attack the drivers.

Edmond rode from the trees on his horse, sword raised, making straight for the leader of the escort. He was a large man, obviously an experienced fighter. Edmond had never been in battle before. He knew he was taking a "foolish risk" against the king's orders, but he felt he was a man now, and this was his chance to prove it.

The Viking wheeled his horse around and swung his sword with immense force. The two swords clashed. Edmond's went spinning away into the bushes, wrenched from his hand by the impact. The Norseman raised his sword again, this time to topple Edmond's head from his shoulders. The two horses were side by side, almost touching. It was no time for the nice tactics that Edmond had learnt as a boy. He drew his dagger and kicked his feet from the stirrups. As the sword swung he threw himself out of his saddle, across the other horse. Grabbing what hold he could with his left hand, he used his right hand, holding the dagger, to stab and stab again at his enemy's body.

They fell together in a heap on the ground. Edmond was half underneath the big man's body. He dragged himself free and leapt back. But the Viking lay still. Edmond grabbed the sword from the man's lifeless hand and turned to fight again.

There was no more fighting to be done. The two Viking soldiers still alive were galloping back down the path to Wilton as fast as their horses could carry them. The rest lay on the ground. Yelling Saxons used their battle axes to shatter the chains which held the prisoners, who whooped with joy as they sprang free.

Very soon the Saxons had vanished as if they had never been there. The Viking horses and all the food and valuables vanished too. Only the empty wagons remained on the dusty road with the still bodies of the soldiers beside them.

A GAME OF CHESS

Proud the Viking banner stands,
And proud is Guthrum now.
King of all the Wessex lands,
To him the Saxons bow.

A TIRED messenger arrived at Chippenham and was admitted to the manor hall. The jarls were enjoying themselves, seated at the trestle tables over the remains of a large meal. They were singing their favourite songs and hurling jokes to one another. Two men were having a mock sword battle by the hearth.

The messenger went to the high chair and bowed to Guthrum.

"What news?" asked Guthrum quietly.

In a low voice that the rest could not hear, the messenger described the ambush at Woodbridge. Guthrum listened in silence. His expression did not change though his face grew a shade darker still. At last he nodded and waved the messenger away. He picked up a cup of wine, about to sip it.

Sigfrid came near, roaring with laughter. "Be of good cheer!" he bawled to Guthrum, slapping him heavily on the shoulder.

Guthrum's body jerked forward and wine spilled out of the cup down his tunic. He thumped the cup on to the table and turned to Sigfrid in fury.

"You will learn to treat your king with more respect!"

His voice, though not loud, seemed to reach every man in the hall. The noisy chatter died away. Sigfrid stepped back as if Guthrum had struck him. His big face went scarlet.

At that moment the goat, which had wandered in through the open door, raised its head and bleated loudly. This was too much for the jarls. They burst into fresh laughter.

Guthrum rose from his chair. His finger trembled as he pointed to the goat. "Remove that animal from my presence!"

The goat was quickly pushed out, but the damage was done. Several of the jarls were still sniggering.

Guthrum's voice echoed from the beams, "Get out of here, all of you. Get out of my sight!"

He grabbed a young jarl nearest to him and hurled him away from the table. There was a growl of anger from the rest. They turned their backs on Guthrum and shuffled out of the hall. The servants fled too. Soon only Guthrum and Sigfrid were left. Guthrum strode to the hearth and stared into the flames.

Sigfrid spoke with dignity. "I have sailed in our ships since I was a lad. I learnt that all our men were equal. We knew our captain and we obeyed him, but no more than that. Must we now cringe to him, like Christians?"

Guthrum took a deep breath. "This is not a ship. It is a kingdom. Our people must learn how to rule and be ruled. Yes, like Christians."

Sigfrid turned away toward the door.

Guthrum licked his thin lips. It was not often he gave way to anger and now he was ashamed of it. "Sigfrid. . . . You don't understand. None of them do. They are celebrating a victory we haven't yet won. Alfred is not beaten. He's only hiding in his marshes till he can bring an army together. When he does so – then we shall fight the real battle."

Sigfrid's face split into a grin as the promise of battle restored his good humour. "If that is so, then the sooner the better. Let him gather all the Saxons he can – they'll make more food for the Raven."

"I need men such as you," said Guthrum, and held out his right arm.

Sigfrid clasped it in friendship. "I'll play you a game of chess and beat you," he declared, as if a battle on a board were better than none at all.

The board was fetched. The game was half-way through before

Guthrum spoke of the report which the messenger had brought him.

"Another ambush?" gasped Sigfrid.

Guthrum nodded. "Twenty men lost, along with their horses and all the supplies. That's the third in a week. We've lost a hundred men in less than a month." He sighed, staring at the chess-board. "How does he do it?"

"You mean Alfred?" asked Sigfrid as he moved one of the pieces.

"Alfred, of course. Hidden away, miles from anywhere, yet he can move his men about, just like that!" Guthrum picked up a pawn and put it down again.

Sigfrid frowned. "The man's a magician. He conjures men out of the air like spirits."

Guthrum shook his head. "No, it is not magic. These Christians are taught that since their king is chosen by god they must obey him even when he has no power to force them. They are also taught to work together and to keep the peace in their land. I sometimes wish our own people were taught the same."

Sigfrid looked up, worried. "Are you suggesting that our gods are not good enough for you any more?"

Guthrum pointed at the chess-board. "It's your move," he said.

Sigfrid forced his attention to the board again, but his mind was not on the game. "It still doesn't make sense to me. Since the king is not among his people, how do they know what he wants them to do?"

"Oh, that is simple enough," said Guthrum. "His messengers move about the country under our noses. He even puts his orders down in writing so that no one makes any mistake."

"In writing!" Sigfrid said it with contempt.

Guthrum nodded. "His messengers carry pieces of parchment like weapons of war."

The big man wrinkled his nose in disgust. "What do you want us to do about it – become Christians?"

Guthrum stared at him calmly. "At least we might learn to read and write."

Edmond returned to Alfred's camp to find it almost deserted. The king, he was told, had gone to lead an attack on a small Viking force and only a few men were left to guard the base. Edmond made up his mind to follow the king and join in the attack, but first he made his way to the camp fire where the women had food ready.

Edwina appeared, bringing the children for their meal. Edmond waved to her. She hesitated for a moment, then remembered that she had forgiven him. She sat beside him on a log.

"What is the king hoping to achieve?" asked Edmond.

"He has taken his men to attack a manor near Sherborne. We had word that there is a small Viking force there. The thane surrendered to Vikings and is co-operating with them."

"One of the traitors?"

Edwina nodded. "The king has passed a sentence of death upon him as an example to others, so now he must look to his enemies for protection."

"Do you think the king will take the manor?"

"Yes. He is being joined by the Alderman of Somerset with some local men, so he should find it easy enough. But he could be in danger if the Vikings hear of it in time. They may try to trap him." She waited while Edmond put the remains of his meal down for Adam, then she asked, "Did your ambush succeed?"

Edmond nodded. She was the first person to whom he was able to tell his story, so he described in detail what had happened. He was proud of his first battle.

Edwina looked thoughtful when he had finished. "So you killed a man?" she said, glancing at him. Edmond seemed very young to be a warrior.

"Yes. I had to kill him, or he would have killed me." Then he admitted, "But I had to kill him anyway. That is what we were there for."

"Yes, of course. It is their own fault. They have brought it upon themselves." She stared thoughtfully at the earth at her feet. "I had a chance once . . . I could have killed Guthrum himself."

Edmond's eyes widened as Edwina described what had happened in the church at Chippenham.

"I couldn't bring myself to do it," said Edwina. "I suppose I ought to be ashamed."

"Killing is not for girls," said Edmond, excusing her. He grinned to show that he didn't blame her. "You're very brave all the same. I'm glad I'm not your enemy."

"I hope we're friends," said Edwina.

Edmond left the camp again that night, making for Sherborne, but when he reached the edge of the forest he met the king returning with his men. They were marching fast to escape from a company of Norsemen who had hurriedly set out from Sherborne itself. Once within the cover of the forest they threw off the pursuit.

They all returned to the camp triumphant. The manor had

been taken and the Viking defenders had been slain. The thane who had given in to his enemies had been executed, and Alfred returned with more men than when he set out. All along the route men who could be spared from their fields had come to join him. It was still a very tiny army, but it was beginning to grow.

A PLACE AND A DATE

The king he sat before the fire,
His heart was deeply aching.
The cowherd's wife said, "Now, good Sire,
Please watch those cakes a-baking."

The king he watched but did not see,
His thoughts to battle turning,
When she came back she said, "Ah me!
You've left the cakes a-burning!"

As the days grew longer buds appeared on the trees of the forest and flocks of birds returned from the southern world to nest among the lakes. For all living things it was a time of preparation.

Soon after Easter Alfred moved his camp on to the highest patch of dry land to be found among the marshes. It was surrounded by water and was known as the Isle of Athelney. Here there was room for the men who came, more and more of them, to join him. Waiting at the camp made them restless and Alfred led them on raids into territory held by the Vikings to keep up their spirits.

He must have been impatient too, though he tried not to show it. Not long after his arrival at Athelney he was laid low with an attack of pain. Some whispered that his illness was brought on by worry about the future. The Alderman of Somerset sent him a book which had come from France. It was beautifully written out by hand in Latin. Alfred laid it on John's writing-board and read it carefully, using a pointer to follow the closely written script. His pain eased.

"I shall have this book translated into English," he said to John. "We'll have as many copies written out as possible."

"As you wish, Sire," said the priest. It was one of Alfred's favourite ideas, that books should be written in English so that as many people as possible might be able to read them.

The faint sound of a lyre came from outside the hut. Alfred laid down his pointer and went to the doorway.

Cedric was seated on a log by the camp fire, composing a new song which described life at the camp. Edwina sat nearby, listening with wonder at his mastery of words. The laughter of the young children could be heard from among the trees.

Ellen appeared beside them with a number of oatmeal cakes set out on a griddle. She placed it carefully over some glowing

embers at the edge of the fire.

"What is the king doing?" asked Edwina.

"Reading a book!" said Ellen. Her tone suggested that a king might find more useful things to do.

Edwina smiled. "His books help to make him wise. I've heard him say that every boy in the kingdom should be taught to read, rich and poor alike."

Cedric stopped playing. "Does he really think that?"

Edwina nodded. "He once told me that some day even girls might learn to read."

This was too much for Ellen. "Girls – learn to read?" she gasped. "I never heard such nonsense in my life."

"I'm glad *I* can read," said Cedric.

Ellen sniffed. "My husband was a poor cowherd. He couldn't read or write, but he was as good a man as any poet – or any king for that matter."

"I can well believe it," said a gentle voice behind her.

Ellen swung round to find Alfred gazing down at her.

"Oh, Sire!" stammered Ellen. "I – I didn't mean—"

Alfred laughed and glanced toward the fire. "I feel hungry today. What have we here? Oatmeal cakes?" He stretched out a hand toward the griddle.

Ellen drew herself up. He might be king of Wessex, but cakes were *her* business. "They are not baked yet, Sire – if you please!"

Alfred drew back his hand and answered gravely. "I do beg your pardon, ma'am. I will wait, if I may."

Ellen gave him a stiff bow and marched off toward the lake.

Cedric had risen from the log and Alfred took his place on it. "You may go on playing," he said.

Cedric raised his hand to the lyre but before he could play a young man strode into view, dressed in rags and looking very tired. It was Edmond. He held a parchment in his hand, rolled and sealed. Edwina felt a stir of excitement. She knew he had been on another mission into Dorset.

Word of his arrival was spreading quickly. Men appeared from all sides, anxious to hear what news he had brought.

Edmond knelt before the king and offered him the parchment. "From the Alderman of Dorset, Sire."

Before opening the roll, Alfred handed it to John. "Is it genuine?" he asked. It was unlikely that the Vikings could have forged a message and put it in the hands of a trusted messenger, but he had to be sure.

John examined it and nodded. "That is the Alderman's seal. And I recognise his clerk's handwriting."

Alfred broke the seal and opened the parchment. There was an expectant silence while he read the message. He gave a nod of satisfaction and spoke loudly enough for them all to hear.

"The Alderman informs me that the men of Dorset are fully armed and ready for battle."

There was a murmur among the men. Messengers had been arriving almost daily from different parts of Wessex with similar news. Edwina whispered eagerly to Cedric, "Now Dorset is ready too! That means every county is prepared for battle."

Cedric shrugged his shoulders. "What use is that? The men may be armed, but they are scattered all over the country."

Alfred was still examining the message. "The Alderman begs permission to attack Chippenham with his force."

This brought gasps from the men and one of the thanes spoke for them, "Not without us, Sire! Let us join him in the attack."

But Alfred shook his head. "The Alderman must not attack

Chippenham with only one small force, not even with our aid." He stared into the fire, deep in thought. At last he said, "The time has come to gather our forces together, from every part of Wessex, to form a single army strong enough to defeat Guthrum."

A cheer rose from the clearing that might have been heard the other side of the lake.

It was followed by a buzz of talk. The men were too excited to return to their tasks around the camp. They were like bows suddenly drawn tight, ready to let the arrows fly. Something was needed to ease the tension, and it came unexpectedly.

"My cakes!" shrieked a voice. Ellen had come back from the lake and was pointing in fury at her oatmeal cakes, burnt black on the griddle.

"You've let them burn," she cried, looking straight at the king. Alfred was still staring into the fire, unaware of what was going on.

The men exploded in a roar of laughter. Alfred looked up, surprised. "What is it?" he asked. "What has happened?"

Cedric stepped forward, raising his lyre. "Hear me, Sire," he said, grinning. "I will tell you what happened."

He plucked the lyre and began to sing slowly, choosing his words as he went along.

"The king he sat before the fire.
His heart was deeply aching.
The cowherd's wife said, 'Now good Sire,
Please watch those cakes a-baking.'

The king he watched but did not see,
His thoughts to battle turning.
When she came back she said, 'Ah me!
You've left the cakes a-burning!' "

Cedric held up the lyre in triumph and a fresh torrent of laughter came from the men.

Alfred shook his head, smiling ruefully. "What foolish tales poets make up out of nothing," he declared. "I hope that no one ever repeats it."

That night Edwina left the women gossiping in their huts and made her way to the camp fire. She stopped in the shadows of the trees at the edge of the clearing where she could watch and listen.

The thanes were gathered around the fire talking in low voices while they waited for the king to appear. A few torches burned on poles to give more light. Edmond was there, sitting apart from the rest. He was sprawled on the ground with his back against a tree trunk. Adam lay beside him, nose between his paws. Edmond's sharp eyes spotted Edwina among the trees. He winked at her. She drew further back, feeling like a child caught spying on her elders.

The men rose to their feet as Alfred came from his hut with John, as always, close behind him. Two guards brought his stool and set it down beneath the pole from which the dragon standard hung. Alfred took his place and waved a hand for the others to sit too. There was breathless silence until he spoke.

"I have decided upon a place and a date when our separate forces shall meet together," he said. "First the place. It must be somewhere easily reached and well known to everyone. Egbert's Stone stands where three counties meet together: Wiltshire, Dorset and Hampshire. That shall be the meeting place."

He paused as the men nodded to one another, then he continued. "As to the date, we must allow time for the order to be sent to every county, for the men to be informed, and for them to make their way to the meeting place. I suggest three weeks from today. That will be—?" He glanced at John.

"The seventh Friday after Easter, Sire," replied the priest.

"So be it. On that day, at Egbert's Stone, I shall take command of my army."

There was a fierce and eager murmur among the men. Edwina felt her own heart quickening with excitement.

"The orders will be sent to each county in writing," Alfred went on. "Our messengers will have a heavy duty to perform. If any one of them should fail it could mean the loss of an entire force."

Edwina glanced at Edmond. He was sitting up straight now, his eyes shining. She felt a deep envy.

Alfred was speaking again. "The aldermen will be told not to march their troops in large companies. Each man must make his own way to the meeting place as secretly as possible, either alone or in small groups, so that the enemy is not warned of what is happening."

Some of the thanes grinned at the notion of an army gathering in secret. "How shall *we* reach Egbert's Stone?" asked one of them.

"Our force will be split up like the rest. We shall take separate paths out of the forest."

"How shall we attack the Vikings?" asked another.

Alfred paused before replying, "They are sure to discover what is going on before we are ready to fight them. Much will depend on what Guthrum plans to do. I wish I had some way of finding out."

Edwina moved softly through the trees toward the king's hut. She barely heard the discussion that followed, too full of her own thoughts. The thanes were asking more questions and making their own suggestions. They were mainly concerned for the safety of the king himself, and Alfred agreed that a bodyguard should escort him.

At last he rose and the men bowed to him. As soon as he had turned away they settled into more talk which looked like lasting half the night.

Alfred paused at the door of the hut, seeing Edwina in the shadows.

"Child, what are you doing here at this time of night?" he asked.

She took a quick step forward and fell on her knees. "Sire, I beg you, give me some task to perform, so that I can be of service too."

Alfred put out a hand and lifted her to her feet. "The women and children will go to Glastonbury. The priests will take care of you, and you will be safe until . . . until the issue is decided."

"But, Sire—"

He raised a hand and his voice was firm. "Your task will be to help with the children, as you have been doing all along. May God protect you, and all of us."

With that he strode into the hut. Edwina clenched her fists. She heard a faint chuckle behind her, and swung round.

"What do you want to do?" asked Edmond. "Lead the battle-charge?"

Edwina turned to him, furious. She wanted to claw his face, but decided that would be too womanish. She couldn't hope to beat him with her fists, so instead she turned and ran. She didn't stop till she had reached the edge of the lake where the moonlight glinted from tiny ripples in the water.

If only she could prove to them all (especially Edmond) that she was capable of more than looking after children!

At that moment she remembered something Alfred had said earlier. "Much will depend on what Guthrum plans to do. *I wish we had some way of finding out!*"

An idea entered Edwina's head, so bold she gasped aloud. It seemed highly dangerous. And yet, the more she thought of it, the more she became sure that it was possible. She returned slowly to the women's huts but she did not sleep until it was nearly morning.

THE SECRET ARMY

King Alfred from his lonely den
On Isle of Athelney
Sends out a call to Saxon men
To set their country free.

To east and west, by night and day,
The secret message goes,
By every trick and cunning way
We hide it from our foes.

Cunning now is what we need
To pass it, hand by hand,
Scattering the words like seed
Throughout the waiting land.

JOHN STOOD at his board writing out the king's order in careful script. He wrote the same message over and over again. As each was completed he rolled the parchment, fastened down the edge with melted wax, and pressed in the royal seal.

Messengers set off, one by one. Edmond grinned cheerfully as John handed him a copy of the order, addressed to the Alderman of Dorset.

"Take good care it does not fall into enemy hands," said John gravely.

"I shall take care," answered Edmond. He mounted his horse. Adam was already running eagerly to the lakeside, aware that a new mission had begun.

Edmond eased the horse into the water which was shallow enough to wade through. Only Adam had to swim across the deepest patch. At the other side Edmond headed south-east along a path he had used before.

He slept that night in the forest, wrapped tightly in the torn and faded cloak which served him also as a blanket, with Adam huddled beside him. At dawn he set off again and emerged from the forest into open country.

Very soon he stopped. A pall of smoke was rising from behind a hill in front of him. There was too much smoke to be caused by an ordinary fire. It looked as if houses were burning. This was quite possible. The Vikings had been driven to fury by their soldiers being killed and their supplies stolen. From time to time they would descend upon some luckless village and burn it to the ground as a punishment.

If so it meant there was a raiding party in the area, and most likely they had come from Dorchester, the town Edmond was heading for. He knew he must take no chances. He called Adam to his side for a few moments. Then he continued his journey at a walking pace, taking a long way round to avoid the village.

The slow pace made him impatient, but he had to give the Norsemen time to return to Dorchester ahead of him. The road entered a wood and Edmond halted, listening. There was no sound but the chirping of birds and the faint rustling of creatures among the tree roots. He moved on, satisfied there was no danger.

He turned a sharp bend and realised his mistake too late. Two spears were raised in front of him, held by Viking soldiers.

"Dismount!" said one. The other called a warning and two other men appeared, one of them an officer.

The Vikings had left a guard to watch the road! Edmond felt his stomach turn sick as he climbed off the horse. This time it was he who had been ambushed.

"Who are you? Why are you travelling?" asked the officer.

"For my master, the Thane of Colbury," answered Edmond promptly. Colbury was a village a little to the north and the thane was one marked out as a traitor. "His aged mother is sick. I am riding to Dorchester as fast as I can. I must consult a wise woman who has a certain cure for the ague." Edmond knew that the thane had an ageing mother, though whether she suffered from ague or not he had no idea.

"Search him," said the officer.

Their hands prodded through Edmond's ragged clothing but they found nothing on him.

"And the horse," said the officer, impatient.

They looked under the saddle and into the saddlebag, where they found the remains of a loaf of bread, some cheese and a wooden bowl. They took the stopper from the leather water-bottle to look inside. It contained only water.

"Let him go," said the officer.

Edmond mounted his horse with relief and set off down the path at a canter. He turned several more bends, then he stopped and whistled.

Adam came running from the trees.

"Good boy," said Edmond.

The precious parchment was inside a leather bag that hung around the dog's neck.

Many people were passing through the tall, narrow gateway into the town. A heavy cart lumbered by, loaded with vegetables. The Viking guards on duty at the gate took no notice of a tattered young man who stumbled by, apparently lame in one leg. He held out a wooden begging bowl to the passers-by. A tall hound dog followed at his heels.

The houses of Dorchester lay close together in huddled streets within the wall that protected them. The only open space was the market square and this was filled with traders. Their goods were laid out on carts and trestle tables. Viking soldiers, off-duty, mingled with the crowd.

The Alderman's house stood at one side of the square. It was larger than the rest, surrounded by a wall with a gate that led into a small courtyard. Two more Viking guards were standing at the entrance. Though the Alderman was still allowed to administer the town he was virtually a prisoner in his own home.

Edmond made no attempt to enter the gate, knowing that the guards would stop him. He squatted on the ground and put his begging bowl in front of him. As people passed he whined pitifully, "Spare a penny for a poor lame man." Someone dropped

a coin in the bowl and Edmond cried, "God bless you, good sir."

An hour passed and no one emerged from the Alderman's gate. Edmond was getting impatient. Then he saw a portly priest, a little barrel of a man, come from the church on the other side of the square. Edmond scrambled to his feet, dragging his "lame" leg after him, and knelt before the priest.

"Give your blessing to the sick, good father," said Edmond, adding softly, "and a message to the Alderman, under the Royal Seal."

If the priest was surprised he showed no sign of it. He raised his fingers over Edmond, making a cross in the air. At the same time his other hand reached down. Edmond drew the parchment from inside his cloak and it quickly disappeared up the sleeve of the priest's robe.

"God will protect the poor and needy," said the priest solemnly, and then whispered: "Take care, lad. They are very suspicious of late."

Then he moved on, making for the Alderman's house. Edmond went back to his place and watched. As the priest was about to enter the gate the guards crossed their spears in front of him. The little priest flung up his head in anger. Edmond could not hear what he was saying but he looked very indignant.

So the Vikings were suspicious of everyone! It was only to be expected. Guthrum must have been aware that with the coming of spring the time of reckoning was near. No doubt he had given orders to his men to keep strict watch.

Suddenly the priest turned from the gate and hurried away, almost at a run. The guards muttered together and, to Edmond's horror, one of them set off after him.

The priest stopped beside one of the trader's stalls, a table laden with earthenware pots. He picked up one of them, a bulbous jug with a long neck, examining it. The guard appeared at his elbow and the priest turned as if startled. With quick movements the guard ran his fingers over the priests' robe, while people nearby watched nervously. Edmond held his breath until the guard stepped back. Evidently he had found nothing. The priest, still looking angry, moved away and the guard went back to the gate.

Edmond stood up in order to keep an eye on the priest amid the crowd in the market. The little man moved about, as if searching for something. At length he stopped beside an elderly woman who was buying vegetables. Edmond guessed that she might be one of the Alderman's household servants. The priest spoke to her. She curtsied and he raised his fingers in the usual blessing.

The woman left her vegetables and went straight to the potter's stall. A Viking soldier was idly picking up the pots, one by one. She elbowed him aside, and grabbed the bulbous jug. She threw two coins into the palm of the trader and hurried off with her purchase.

Edmond held his breath again as she approached the Alderman's gate. But she marched past the guards without a glance at either of them, and they ignored her. The jug with its precious contents disappeared into the courtyard.

Edmond waited several days in Dorchester, in case the Alderman should send for him, but no word came. He began to wonder if the message had had any effect. Servants came and went from the Alderman's house, but there was no way of telling if they carried news, and Edmond dared not ask. Still worried, he left the town. He stumbled up the road, pretending to be lame, till he reached the nearest woods. It was there he had left his horse in the safe keeping of some charcoal burners.

He found them putting on cloaks and leggings.

"You're just in time," said their chief. "We are leaving here."

"Leaving?" asked Edmond.

"We got orders from the Alderman yesterday. Every fighting man is to meet King Alfred at Egbert's Stone. Didn't you know?"

"Yes," admitted Edmond with relief, "I did know."

Alfred's camp on the Isle of Athelney looked as if it had been ransacked by Vikings. The huts had been emptied. The fires were dying out. Men were moving about in all directions, collecting weapons and stores. Alfred himself gave orders that his books were to be kept safely, then he knelt to pray in front of the portable altar which went wherever he travelled. The pains which he dreaded so much had suddenly returned. He prayed to God to deliver him from them during the vital days to come.

The women were gathering beside their own huts, awaiting a small guard of foot-soldiers who would escort them to Glastonbury. Edwina handed the children over to their mothers and looked around for Ellen. She found her at the main camp fire, gathering up the cooking pots (just as important to an army as axes and shields). Edwina paused uncertain how to say what was on her mind.

"What are you doing here, child?" asked Ellen. "Well, don't stand there gaping. Since you are here, you can help." She held open a large sack. "Put things in here for the pack-horse to carry."

Edwina obeyed mechanically. "Alfred won't let me go with him into battle," she said.

"Into battle! I should think not!"

Edwina put another pot into the sack, then she stood up. A

high-born lady should not hesitate. She should speak out. "I shall go to Chippenham instead."

The sack fell from Ellen's hand with a clatter of pots. "To Chippenham!" she gasped. "But you can't go there. Are you out of your mind?"

Edwina's worried look had gone. Her eyes shone brightly. "I'm not out of my mind. I *must* do it. Guthrum will know by now what is happening. He will be making plans to meet Alfred's attack. We can find out what his plans are, and think of some way to warn the king."

Ellen's mouth opened and closed several times before she managed to repeat, "*We* can find out? What do you mean – we?"

Edwina spoke quickly but firmly. "You must come with me, Ellen. We left Chippenham together, and we must go back together. We'll say that we got lost in the forest. That's true enough. We *did* get lost."

Ellen shook her head in disbelief. "How can you say we've been lost in a forest all this time? It's been months!"

"That's true," Edwina admitted. The idea of spying on Guthrum had so excited her she had not thought out all the details. "We'll say that someone found us and looked after us. We do need someone to help us, someone who can guide us through the forest." She paused as the sound of a lyre reached them from among the trees. "Cedric, of course!" she whispered.

Cedric wandered into view, rehearsing a song to suit the occasion, though for once no one was taking any notice of him.

"Sharpen axe and polish sword,
Commend thy soul unto the lord.
The day of reckoning is come."

"Cedric!" called Edwina sweetly.

He looked up, annoyed by the interruption. "What do you want?"

"*You* may be able to help us."

Ellen threw up her hands. "Him! A fine protector he'll make!"

Edwina sighed, looking from one to the other. Weak allies, both of them, but all she had. "Are you going into battle with the king?" she asked.

Cedric seemed surprised by the question. "Me? He won't let me. He says I would scare him more than the enemy."

"Good," said Edwina. "In that case you can guide us home instead."

Cedric shrugged his shoulders. "Very well, if you wish." He raised his lyre, about to play it again. Then it dawned on him. "Home! But your home is Chippenham!"

"Yes," said Edwina calmly.

"Where Guthrum is – and half the Viking army!"

"That is why we are going there, to spy on them."

Cedric's jaw dropped like Ellen's had done. "Spy on—?"

"You want to serve Alfred, don't you?"

"Yes – I mean, no. I mean, not like that. I'm no use as a spy. I'm a coward, you know I am." Edwina was staring at him with a look so determined that he backed away. "I can't do it! I won't! I won't—!"

By nightfall they were crossing the marshes, heading east toward Chippenham. Edwina rode on her white pony, head held high, eyes bright with triumph. Ellen moved slowly in front of her on the donkey. Even now she was not sure how Edwina had persuaded her to make the journey. Perhaps because she was a servant, Edwina was her mistress, and God had ordained that one should obey the other.

Cedric rode a short distance ahead, guiding them. The fears in his mind so terrified him that he sang to stifle them.

> "O, who will win the victory,
> And who will bear the loss?
> Which banner will triumphant be,
> The Raven or the Cross?"

The Whispering Air

The whispering air in Guthrum's hall
Foretells a clash of kings.
The Raven hears the battle call
And stirs its angry wings.

The Saxon men are marching, Sire.
King Alfred claims his own.
You who set this land on fire
Must now defend your throne.

EDWINA urged her pony over the brow of the hill and stopped, looking down at the Manor of Chippenham. When she had left it only two Viking companies had been camped around the stockade. Now there were five times as many tents overflowing on to the village fields.

She waved to Cedric and Ellen who were following her. "Look down there," she cried, "the whole Viking army must be here, or most of it anyway."

Cedric's face turned pale at the sight. "Why are they all at Chippenham?" he asked.

"Guthrum is no fool," replied Edwina. "He knows that Alfred is gathering an army. He has called his own companies back here, ready for battle."

She urged her pony on again, moving down the hill, but soon realised that the other two were not following. "Come on," she called.

Cedric shook his head. "I'm not going down there. I brought you here as you asked me to. If you want to spy on the Vikings may God go with you. I shall not."

"But, Cedric," cried Edwina, "you've come so far you can't run away now."

"Oh, yes, I can," he said, and pulled the horse's head around.

"Hold on!" Ellen called to him. "I'm coming with you." She turned the donkey round.

"Ellen, please! I need your help!" The thought of facing Guthrum on her own was too much even for Edwina.

"I'm not putting my head in that lion's mouth," said Ellen. "Not even for King Alfred."

The horse and the donkey began to move away. Tears of anger filled Edwina's eyes. "You're cowards, both of you. Cowards and traitors! I'll never forgive you! I'll—"

She got no further. Cedric and Ellen had pulled up. Coming over the hill straight in front of them was a party of jarls, returning from their hunt.

Guthrum sat in the manor hall listening to a report that a messenger had brought him. At length he nodded. "So Alfred has left his hiding place at last. Where did you see him?"

"On the border of Somerset, heading east into Dorset," replied the messenger. "He had a bodyguard with him. We knew who they were by the banners they carried. One was the Dragon of Wessex and the other had a cross on it. We were only a few men so we dared not attack. We drew off, and I rode here at once."

"You have done well," said Guthrum. He turned to Osric. "What of the other reports?"

"They all tell the same story, Sire," said Osric. "Saxon men on the move all over Wessex, travelling mostly by night, and trying to hide from our men. There's no way of knowing how many, but the few we have captured have all been armed for battle."

"Armed for battle . . ." repeated Guthrum quietly. "They are going to meet Alfred. We can be sure of that."

"I do not see how we can stop them," said Osric. "We would need thousands of men to guard every path, and most of our companies are here at Chippenham now."

There was a loud thump as Sigfrid crashed his fist on to a table. His deep voice growled, "Let him have his army! Let him meet us in open battle! We'll show them who is king!"

Guthrum looked at the big man calmly. "We are all as eager as you are to settle this matter once and for all, but—" He gripped the arms of the chair in his long, thin hands. "The battlefield must be of *our* choosing!"

He rose from his chair and began to pace up and down. "We need more information. We must know where Alfred is meeting his men, and which direction he intends to move after that."

"Perhaps this could tell us, Sire," said Osric. He took a rolled parchment from inside his tunic. "One of the prisoners we took was carrying it."

"What is it?" asked Sigfrid, eyeing the parchment doubtfully.

"We think it is one of Alfred's orders to his officers. You see, it carries his seal."

Guthrum took the parchment. The circle of wax had been broken in order to open the roll, but the pattern of the seal on the two halves was still clear.

"Well? What does it say?" asked Sigfrid impatiently.

Guthrum offered him the parchment. "Perhaps you'll read it for us?"

Sigfrid stepped back as if Guthrum had pointed a dagger at at him. "Read it? How can I read it?"

Guthrum turned to Osric. "Fetch the prisoner who was carrying it. He can be made to read it for us."

Osric looked uncomfortable. "Sire, the man is dead. Our soldiers were under orders to kill all prisoners." He glanced at Sigfrid whose cheeks turned even redder than usual.

"Your order?" asked Guthrum.

"How was I to know?" spluttered the big man. "You said we must strike terror into the Saxons. You said—"

"Yes, yes, yes!" Guthrum waved him to silence and spoke to Osric again. "There must be someone in the village who can read – a clerk, perhaps?"

"I imagine so," agreed Osric. "But no one will admit to it."

Guthrum's voice grated angrily. "Someone must be found!"

As he said it several jarls came in from the courtyard with their hunting spears. After them came Edwina, Ellen and Cedric guarded by soldiers.

"We found these Saxons on the hill," explained one of the jarls. "We thought you might like to question them."

Guthrum's eyes stared piercingly at Edwina and Ellen, whom he recognised, and at Cedric whose canvas bag hung over his shoulder with the lyre in it. "Yes, I do wish to question them!" He pointed a finger at Edwina. "I gave you permission to go to Mildenhall, to be married. I have since been told that you never got there. Where have you been?"

"I can explain, Sire," said Edwina. "When Ellen and I left Chippenham we took a wrong turning in the woods, and we got lost."

"Lost?" repeated Guthrum. "Have you been 'lost' all this time?"

"Not all the time," admitted Edwina. She pointed to Cedric. "This young man found us and he looked after us. We would have returned to Chippenham earlier, but Ellen has been very ill."

Ellen coughed wheezily, but it was not very impressive. Edwina continued quickly, "As soon as she was well enough we came back to ask your forgiveness."

"How very touching," said Guthrum icily. He turned his gaze on to Cedric. "And who are you?"

Cedric was too frightened to find words. "I – I – I—"

"His name is Cedric," said Edwina hastily. "He is a poet. A very good poet, aren't you?"

Cedric nodded.

"A poet, eh?" Guthrum's eyes narrowed. "We Norsemen are lovers of poetry. Is that a harp of some kind?" He pointed to the canvas bag.

"M-my lyre," agreed Cedric. "D-do you wish me to play?"

Guthrum put an arm round Cedric's shoulders, as if in friendship. "They tell me that Saxon poets often write down their verses, so that people will not forget them."

"Y-yes." Cedric nodded again. "I do that sometimes."

"You are trembling," said Guthrum, which was true. Cedric's knees were shaking. "Are you so eager to serve me?"

"Oh yes, Sire. I will serve you in any way I can."

"Good! You can do so now." Guthrum drew his parchment roll from under his cloak. "You can read this for me."

Cedric's eyes widened in dismay at the sight of Alfred's seal. Edwina gave a tiny gasp. Ellen closed her eyes, wishing she were anywhere in the world but Chippenham.

For a moment there was silence and Guthrum waved the parchment. "Did you hear what I said? You needn't set it to music. We'll hear it as it is."

Cedric had stopped trembling. Words burst out of him. "I was lying. I can't read. I'm – I'm not a poet at all."

A loud "Ha!" came from Sigfrid whose patience never lasted very long. His hand reached out and took an axe that hung on one of the oak pillars. "Leave him to me. I'll teach him to read!"

Cedric gave a gasp of terror. Guthrum shook his head sadly. He handed the parchment to Osric and strode away to the hearth, as if he wanted nothing more to do with the matter.

Sigfrid nodded to the soldiers. They took hold of Cedric's right arm and thrust it on to the table, holding it firmly.

Sigfrid raised the axe over Cedric's wrist. "If ever you want to play your lyre again you will tell me what is written in that message."

Osric opened the parchment and held it up so that Cedric could see it. Cedric's breath came out in faint whispers but no words formed. Edwina closed her eyes, unable to watch.

Sigfrid raised the axe a fraction higher and his voice boomed, "Where is Alfred meeting his men?"

Sweat poured down Cedric's face. He heaved at his arm but it was pinned fast to the table. At last his voice sounded faintly.

"I can't tell you! I can't!"

Sigfrid's face went pale with anger. He raised the axe higher, about to bring it down.

There was a sudden shriek. "Look! The Raven! Its wings are moving!" It was Ellen who cried out, pointing at the Raven banner.

They all turned their heads. Even Cedric looked up at the banner. The embroidered wings were fluttering gently.

Sigfrid's eyes grew wide. "An omen!" he growled. "What does it mean?"

He was answered with a faint laugh. It came from Guthrum who was eyeing all of them with contempt. "It means that the door is open, and the draught is stirring the banner – that is all!"

Sigfrid's face turned red again.

Cedric slumped into the arms of the soldiers who were holding him.

"He has fainted," said Osric.

Guthrum strode back toward them. "The man is an idle boaster, and a coward too. Of course he can't read, or he would have done so in the first place."

Edwina stared at Guthrum with relief and surprise. Did he

really think that? Or was he glad of an excuse to stop the torture? Perhaps the Viking chief was not as savage as most of his followers. Perhaps she had been right not to kill him that day in the church. . . .

"Take them away. Lock them up," said Guthrum.

Cedric was carried away by the soldiers. Edwina and Ellen followed. Sigfrid gave vent to his feelings by bringing down the axe with a great thud, on to the empty table-top.

At Egbert's Stone

From Devon farms and Hampshire towns
The tide of Wessex flows.
At Egbert's Stone on Dorset downs
The Saxon army grows.

From Wiltshire and from Somerset
Come forth the noble lords.
At Alfred's banner they are met
To offer him their swords.

CEDRIC opened his eyes. It was dark but he could see Edwina's face peering down at him. From under the floor on which he was lying he heard the muffled sound of a horse whinnying.

"He's awake," said Edwina.

Ellen's face came into view. "Are you all right?" she asked.

Cedric managed to nod. He remembered the axe held over his wrist and raised his arm in panic. It was still in one piece. "What happened?" he asked.

"Guthrum let you go after you fainted," said Edwina.

Cedric raised himself on one elbow, looking at them anxiously. "That message – it was one of Alfred's orders for his men to meet him at Egbert's Stone. Did I – did I tell them—?"

Edwina shook her head, smiling at him proudly. "No, you didn't! They were going to cut off your right hand, yet you wouldn't read the message."

Cedric sank back in the straw with relief.

"I don't understand it," said Ellen. "If you're such a coward, why didn't you read it for them?"

Cedric looked up at them again, puzzled. "I don't understand it either. I would have done anything they asked, but . . ." He spread his hands helplessly. "I couldn't do *that*, could I?"

Edwina smiled again. "You only *think* you're a coward. You're not really."

The horse whinnied again, down below. "Where are we?" asked Cedric.

"We're in the loft over the stable," Edwina explained. "They've shut us in here. Guthrum doesn't trust me any more."

"Which is not surprising," added Ellen.

Cedric sat up, looking angry. "So much for your clever ideas! You bring us here to spy on the Vikings and look at us now.

We're prisoners!"

"Don't be so sure of that," said Edwina. "It's not the first time I've been shut in here." She rose to her feet and went to the doorway. "Remember when I was little, Ellen? You used to put me in here when I was naughty." She put her shoulder against the big door but it would not move.

"I remember," said Ellen grimly. "And you won't open that. There's wooden bars on the other side."

"I know," said Edwina. "That's why I had to find another way out."

"Another way out?" Ellen rose to her feet. So did Cedric, bending his head to avoid the roof beams.

Edwina was peering behind some big sacks of grain that were stored in the loft. "Yes, the ladder is still here."

"Ladder? What ladder?"

"You never knew about it, did you?" said Edwina, smiling. "You didn't know about this either." She bent down in the middle of the floor, pulling the straw aside to reveal a wooden panel let into the planks. "This is how I used to escape."

She gripped an iron ring and pulled it. Slowly the panel rose. All three of them peered down through the opening into the stable below. They could see some of the horses in their stalls.

"I always got back before suppertime, when you came to fetch me," explained Edwina. "You never knew I'd been out all day."

"Well, upon my soul!" gasped Ellen.

Cedric grabbed the ring out of Edwina's hand and lowered the panel back into place. "You're not going down there," he said firmly.

"But I must—"

"No! You've risked our lives once too often. If you try to spy on them now you'll be caught. Guthrum will have you put to death at once – and me too!"

"But you can't stop me—"

"Oh, yes, I can!" Cedric seated himself on top of the panel. "Tell me I'm a coward if you like, but I'm not letting you go."

"And quite right, too!" said Ellen. She seated herself beside Cedric. "At least if we stay here and keep quiet we'll be safe for a while."

Edwina looked at them both, too furious to say anything.

Guthrum came from the manor hall. Sigfrid strode at his side wearing his riding cloak.

"Just find out where Alfred's army is, and where he intends to lead them," said Guthrum.

"I'll find out soon enough," replied Sigfrid. He swung himself into the saddle of the big horse that stood waiting for him.

Guthrum looked up at him. "I don't like the idea of your riding alone."

"I shall ride faster alone," said Sigfrid grimly. "Have no fear. I shan't let the Saxons kill me before I can meet them in battle."

Without more words he dug his heels into the horse's flanks and clattered over the courtyard. Guthrum watched him ride out of the gate.

Sigfrid headed due south as fast as he could go. Osric had carefully pieced together all the reports which told of Saxons moving across the country, and it seemed they were heading for a point somewhere in the far south of Dorset. Sigfrid made no attempt to hide himself. In a country full of hostile people it might have seemed a reckless way to travel. But since the Saxons had no idea he was coming they could not prepare an ambush,

and he relied on his speed to keep him out of trouble.

He took care at night, keeping well off the road in a thick wood. The next morning he rubbed wet mud over his helmet, and pushed his richly patterned sword hilt out of sight under his cloak. There was now little to distinguish him from any Saxon thane who might be riding to join his king.

By midday he knew that he was nearing the southern boundary of the county and again he drew off the road, travelling along the edge of woodland which would give him shelter if he needed it. At last he saw what he was looking for – Saxon men moving across the road in front of him, heading east. They were no longer travelling singly. There was a whole company of them, confident that they were now safe from a Viking attack.

Sigfrid turned into the wood to follow their path without being seen. An hour later he reached the far edge of the wood and stopped abruptly.

In front of him the ground sloped in a shallow vale that was covered with men as far as the eye could reach. All were facing the higher ground on the other side. On the crest of the hill stood the stone erected long ago by King Egbert to mark the boundaries of three counties. Beside it, on horseback, sat a tall figure with a ginger beard. On either side of Alfred stood his senior officers and over their heads fluttered two banners, the dragon and the cross.

A cheer rang out from the waiting men as the latest company marched into their midst. The officer in charge of it, a man of high rank, strode up to Alfred and kneeled in front of him. Alfred held out his hand and the Alderman put his lips to it as a sign of loyalty.

An hour passed while more men arrived to join the host

already there. The shadows were lengthening over the vale as Alfred raised his arms and a trumpet sounded. Sigfrid, hidden among the trees, strained forward to listen like everyone else.

Alfred's voice was not powerful but he spoke slowly and carefully so that his words carried clearly on the faint breeze.

"I call on every one of you to fight beside me. But I ask you not to fight on my account alone. Though I be king, Wessex is yours as well as mine. I call on you to fight for your homes and your families." His voice rose a fraction higher. "Behold – a pack of wolves has come to Wessex. The wolves kill your sheep and murder your children. Join me, with faith in your hearts and steel in your hands, and we will be rid of these wolves for ever!"

A great burst of cheering answered him. Spears rose like an iron-tipped forest and the men stamped their feet on the ground. The king raised an arm again and the noise died away.

"Tomorrow we begin our march. We shall march north, to attack our enemy at Chippenham."

This time the cheering was even more frenzied. Sigfrid did not wait until it ended. He knew all he needed to know. He moved his horse back through the trees as fast as he could. The cheering continued to ring in his ears as if he would never escape from it.

It was early in the morning when Sigfrid got back to Chippenham. He had ridden all through the night practically without stopping and he was very tired, but he strode into the manor hall with a grin of triumph on his face.

The jarls were already risen from the benches around the walls, where they slept. They were honing their swords sharp enough to cut off a man's beard, and polishing them till they gleamed. The hall was tense with their impatience.

Guthrum came hurrying from his private quarters. He clasped

Sigfrid's arm in eager welcome.

"You bring me news?" he asked.

Sigfrid nodded, sitting himself wearily on a bench. "Alfred is due south of here, about two days' march away. His army is with him. He starts moving northward this morning. He means to attack us here, at Chippenham."

The jarls burst into excited chatter. This was the news they had been waiting for. Guthrum's eyes gleamed too, but he remained silent, in deep thought.

"What will we do?" Sigfrid asked him. "Shall we wait for him here?"

Guthrum shook his head. "No. If we wait here Alfred will have the advantage of the hills around us. He will be able to charge downhill and we shall have to fight uphill. It has always been my belief that whoever has the high ground has half the battle won."

He turned to a table beside him and picked up two sharpened daggers that lay on it. He jabbed both the daggers into the table-top, some distance apart. They stood upright on their points, swaying like banner-poles.

"We are here, at Chippenham," said Guthrum, pointing to the dagger on his left. Then he pointed to the other one. "There is Alfred, due south of us. Is there anywhere in between where we might—?"

"Yes, there is!" roared Sigfrid. He took his own sword and laid it across the table near to the left-hand dagger. "There's a ridge of high ground near the village of Edington, only a few hours march from here. I passed it on my way. Alfred must pass it too if he is coming here."

"Excellent!" said Guthrum. He turned to his jarls. "We will take possession of the ridge before Alfred reaches it. Then *we* shall fight downhill. Warn your men that we shall march at dawn tomorrow. And tell them that before the day is out our enemies will be destroyed!"

RACE TO BATTLE

The hills and dales of Wessex ring
To sound of marching feet.
Viking Chief and Saxon King
Will soon in battle meet.

Onward 'neath the rising sun,
Over heath and moor,
To gain the ridge at Edington,
To win the race of war.

EDWINA crouched by the door of the loft listening to the sounds from outside.

"They seem to be rushing about a lot," she reported. "I wish I knew what they were up to."

Cedric was examining a half-loaf of bread. Twice a day the guards brought them food, mostly left-overs from the meals in the hall. "This isn't clean," he decided, and threw it down in the straw. Then he answered Edwina. "I don't see that it matters what they are up to, so long as they leave us alone. Even if you knew what was happening, there's nothing you can do about it, so what is the point of—?"

"Ssh!" whispered Edwina fiercely. "There's someone coming into the stable." She threw herself to the floor, putting an ear to one of the many cracks between the planks.

A voice reached her clearly from below. "You will leave at once. You'll take the road to Winchester and ride as fast as you can."

"It's Osric," whispered Edwina, "he's giving an order to one of his men."

Cedric and Ellen looked at one another, then both put their ears down to the planks.

"You'll meet the ninth company on its way back to Chippenham," Osric continued.

"What am I to tell them?" asked another voice.

"Explain that the army is leaving here at dawn tomorrow. We are marching south. There is a ridge of high ground just beyond the village of Edington. We intend to take possession of the ridge before Alfred reaches it. Tell the company commander he must march his men with all speed to join us at the ridge. Is that clear?"

The man must have nodded. Osric's voice grew fainter as he

moved to the door of the stable. "I'll warn the men at the gate that you're leaving."

Edwina raised her head and whispered to the others, "The ridge at Edington! The king must be told!"

Cedric and Ellen looked at one another in dismay. Cedric whispered fiercely to Edwina. "That's impossible! If you try to escape from here you'll be stopped before you reach the gate."

"But they won't stop *him*," hissed Edwina, pointing downward. "They'll let the messenger go without question."

"What are you suggesting?" asked Cedric, though he must have guessed what she meant for his face went pale again.

Edwina had already grasped the iron ring. She raised the panel in the floor very gently so that it made no noise and beckoned to Cedric.

They could see the soldier standing in one of the stalls below, saddling his horse. He was a short, stocky man, hardly taller than Edwina. He pulled the strap of the saddle tight, and adjusted the length of the stirrups. Then he moved out of the stall, passing directly underneath the opening on his way to the end of the stable where the equipment was stored.

Edwina pointed to one of the big sacks of grain close beside them, and then pointed through the opening.

Cedric's eyes widened in horror and he shook his head.

Edwina's lips formed the words, "We've got to do it!" She grasped the neck of one of the sacks, trying to drag it forward. Cedric hesitated a moment longer, then he moved forward to help her.

Ellen watched, holding her breath.

The footsteps of the soldier could be heard, returning from the end of the stable. He was carrying a saddlebag. The heavy sack

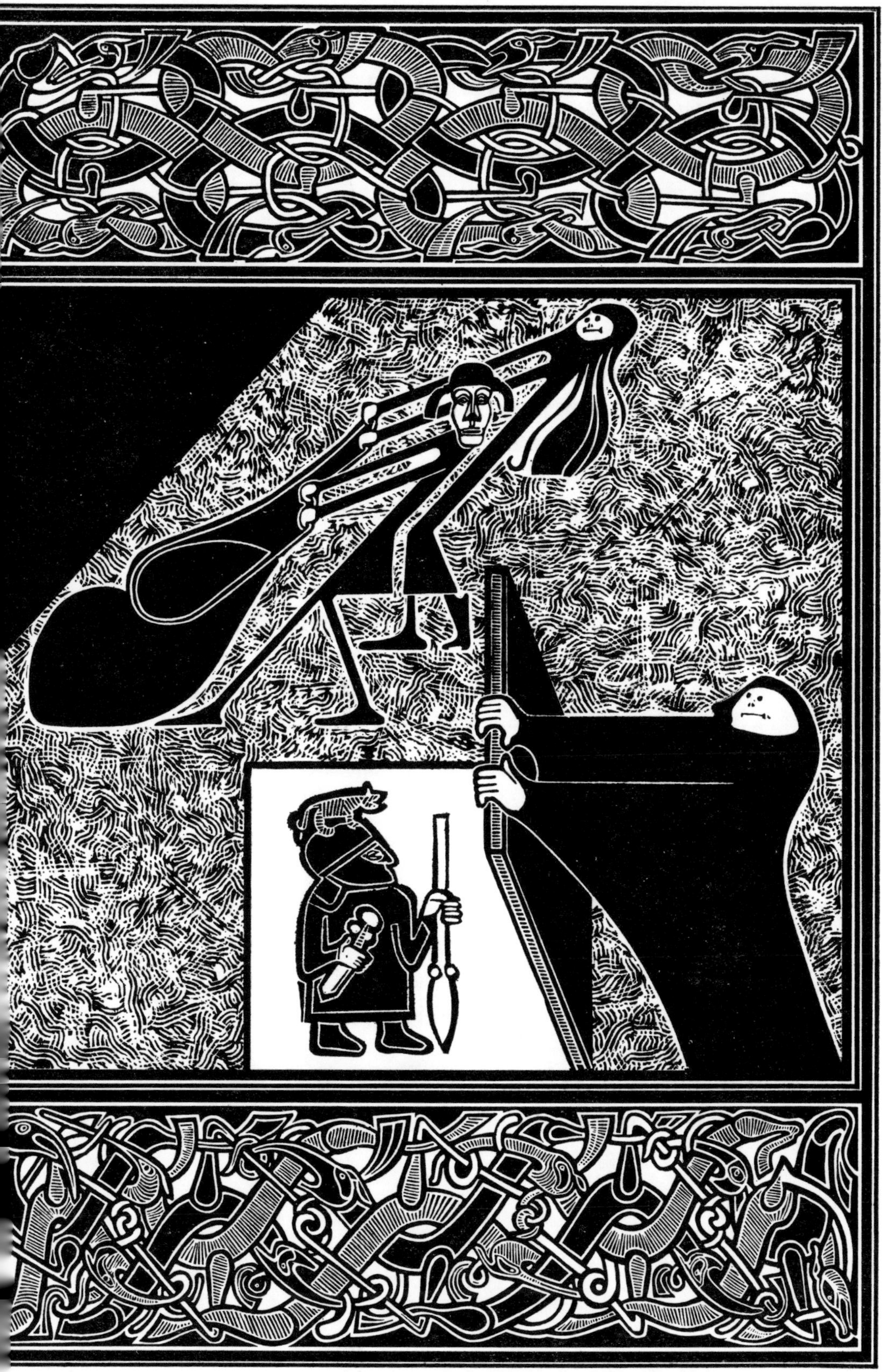

made a scraping noise as it was dragged over the planks above his head. He passed beneath the opening and looked up.

"Now!" cried Edwina, aloud.

The man's upturned face was blotted from view as the sack tottered over the edge. All they heard was the start of a cry, ending in a loud "crump".

Then Cedric leapt through the opening. There was another thump as he landed on the sack and the man lying beneath it. Edwina was already dragging the ladder forward.

A few minutes later the soldier lay in the straw on the loft floor. His wrists and ankles were bound with leather harness straps, and a gag was tucked into his mouth. Ellen stood over him with the prong of a large pitchfork at his throat.

"One move and you die," she said as fiercely as she could. "It is thanks to our Christian mercy that you are still alive."

In the stable Edwina was saddling the horse. She was wearing the soldier's clothes.

"No one will miss him," she said to Cedric. "They will think he has left with his message. When the guards bring you food you must keep him hidden behind the sacks."

"I hope we can keep him quiet," said Cedric doubtfully.

"We should have killed him," said Edwina. Cedric shuddered. They both knew they could not bring themselves to do it.

Edwina scooped earth from the floor of the stable and rubbed it over her face, so that her features looked dark and rough. She put the soldier's helmet over her head and it covered her hair. Then she led the horse to the stable door.

"Pray for me," she said.

"I shall!" nodded Cedric.

Outside the stable Edwina mounted the horse and urged it into a fast trot across the courtyard. She saw the guards at the gate turn as she approached. She made no attempt to pull up.

"It's the messenger," cried one of the guards, and they stood back. One of them shouted as she passed, "May the gods ride with you."

Edwina did not reply but inwardly she thanked him for his good wishes. The horse's hooves thudded over the bridge across the ditch and she passed the Viking tents at a canter. She did not pause until she reached the top of the hill, safely out of Chippenham. Then she pulled the helmet off her head. It was much too big for comfort. She threw it away in the tall grass and let her hair blow out in the wind. Then she spurred the horse into a gallop, heading south.

All that day Alfred rode ahead of his army as they marched steadily northward. When dusk fell he gave orders that the men should make camp for the night. Sentries were posted. Fires were lit. A meal was brought for Alfred who ate with his officers around him, after which they laid themselves on the rough ground, wrapped in their cloaks.

It was pitch dark when a warning shout came from the sentries. Alfred, not yet asleep, sent one of his officers to find out what was happening. He returned to say that the sentries had stopped an intruder. At first they had thought it was a Viking soldier, then they discovered it was a young girl.

"A girl?" said the king, mystified.

The guards appeared, dragging Edwina with them. She fell on her knees at Alfred's feet.

"Edwina!" he gasped. "In heaven's name what are you doing here—?"

Edwina interrupted him with a torrent of words in which "Guthrum's army" and "the ridge at Edington" were jumbled up with explanations.

"Slowly!" commanded Alfred. "Say everything clearly so that I can understand."

Edwina began again. When she had finished for the second time Alfred called to his officers, "Rouse the men at once!"

There were some gasps of astonishment. "But, Sire, you said they could rest—"

"There'll be no rest. We shall march at once. We shall march all night. Pray God we shall march fast enough!"

The men rose grumbling from their sleep and soon the tramp of feet was heard again on the dark road.

Edmond was riding at the head of a party of men from his own manor. Like everyone else he was puzzled by the sudden change of plan. He rode down the column to the front to find out what was happening. He was astonished to see Edwina there, riding beside John, the priest. He pulled his horse alongside hers and she smiled at his look of surprise. Then she told him her story.

"You take more foolish risks than I do," he confessed. "But I understand why the king is in such a hurry to move on." They rode a little while in silence, then Edmond spoke again in a tone of deep respect, "It seems you have led the battle-charge after all!"

The black night still lay over Chippenham as the Viking soldiers collected their weapons and left their tents. In the first grey light of dawn Guthrum rode from the stockade with his jarls.
The men cheered as they saw him. Very soon they had begun their march south.

When the villagers emerged from their homes they found only

empty tents, the ashes of the camp fires, and silence. Their conquerors had gone.

Cedric was wide awake in the loft over the stable. He had hardly slept, being worried by the presence of the prisoner beside him. In fact the man, scared for his life, had made no attempt to attract attention. Cedric put his head to the door, listening. There was no sound anywhere. He raised the panel in the floor. All the horses were gone from the stable. He lowered the ladder. When he stuck his head out of the door there was no one to be seen.

He found some servants crouched beside the hearth in the hall.

"Guthrum has gone," they told him. "He has taken the whole army with him. He has not even left a guard here."

Cedric hurried back to the loft and shook Ellen. "Wake up. The Vikings have gone. We can escape from here."

"Escape?" said Ellen sleepily.

"Remember those other soldiers who are coming from Winchester," said Cedric. "The messenger never reached them, so they will come here. We had better not wait for them."

"You are right," said Ellen. "We will go north and hide in the woods until –" she hesitated – "until the matter has been settled."

Cedric nodded. He looked round. The soldier was looking at him appealingly. Cedric strode over to him, took the gag from his mouth and unfastened his wrists.

"I advise you to stay here and keep very quiet," Cedric told him. "If the village people find you they will surely put you to death. Wait until your comrades arrive, and you can join them."

The soldier nodded gratefully.

"I know I should kill you myself, but I just can't do it," said Cedric, as if apologising. "It's because I'm a coward. You do understand, don't you?" Then he followed Ellen down the ladder.

Clash of Arms

I saw two noble kings arrayed
In cloth of blue and gold.
I saw a thousand men parade
Beneath the banners bold.

I heard a trumpet loudly sound,
I heard a battle cry.
I heard the horses stamp the ground
And arrows softly fly.

I watched the lines of men advance
Across the trembling field.
Pointed spear and thrusting lance
And shield entwined with shield.

A thousand men in mortal fray,
Heaping blow on blow,
Every man intent to slay
Another man, his foe.

GUTHRUM rode ahead of his army with several of his jarls. They emerged from a wood and halted.

"Edington is over there," said Sigfrid, sweeping his arm toward the east. Then he pointed straight ahead. "There is the ridge."

The ground rose in front of them, gently at first, then more steeply. Guthrum shaded his eyes, looking at the brow of the hill. "We will wait here till the rest catch up. How long, do you think, before Alfred can get this far?"

Sigfrid shrugged his big shoulders. "If he marched all yesterday and started again this morning, he should reach the other side of the ridge before the day is out. We have plenty of time to rest our men and make ourselves ready."

Guthrum nodded slowly. "All the same, I shall be more content when our army is up there on the hill."

As if to reassure him, a horn sounded in the wood. The leading company was drawing near. Guthrum glanced over his shoulder, then looked at Sigfrid. "A few hours more and Wessex will be ours for ever. A new Viking kingdom, the biggest and most powerful in Britain. When Alfred has been defeated there will be no one to challenge us."

Sigfrid smiled broadly. He looked up at the ridge. The smile slowly faded from his lips. "What is that?" he asked.

Guthrum shaded his eyes again. Something was fluttering on the top of the ridge. It looked like a banner. Then a line of horsemen came into view. Guthrum and Sigfrid watched in silence, unable to believe their eyes. As the standard-bearers on the hilltop wheeled aside the emblems on their banners glinted plainly in the sun – the Dragon and the Cross. A tall, broad man sat on the leading horse, looking steadily down the hill at them.

"Alfred!" breathed Guthrum, so softly that his lips hardly

moved.

Sigfrid was shaking his head desperately. "It cannot be – he has ridden ahead of his men – those horsemen are his bodyguard – no more than that—"

But even as he said it, the spears of the foot-soldiers began to appear against the bright sky, spreading out along the ridge like reeds at the edge of a lake.

Sigfrid blinked his eyes as if hoping that the Saxons would disappear. "I don't understand! They must have marched all night, as if they knew. . . ." He stopped, glancing at his chief.

Guthrum's face was deathly white. His knuckles too were white, clenching the reins.

Alfred dismounted from his horse still staring at the valley below. He saw the Raven banner hanging limply in the still air at the foot of the slope.

"The race is won," he said softly.

John, beside him, nodded. "Praise be to God."

One by one the Viking companies appeared from the wood, behind Guthrum, spreading out either side of their chief to form a battle line. Alfred looked along the ridge. His own men were forming a line too, led by their thanes.

Alfred turned away from the brow of the ridge. The portable altar had been set up behind the line and Alfred knelt to pray in front of it. No Christian king could go into battle without first commending his soul to God. He gave thanks in his heart that he would be able to fight from a position of strength. He was thankful too because the pains which had troubled him during the journey had vanished in the sight of the enemy.

Meantime the Norsemen made their own preparations. They

killed a rabbit and examined its insides for omens.

"Odin will give strength to our arms," said Sigfrid. But Guthrum did not answer.

Edwina waited impatiently several hundred yards behind the ridge, where the army had dumped its supplies. She was under strict orders to remain in the rear and dared not go forward while Alfred could catch sight of her. She could see him praying at his altar. Beyond him his men were strung out along the ridge top. She heard John intoning a prayer in a loud voice. The Saxons bowed their heads and called "Amen".

Men came down the hill leading the horses on which Alfred and his thanes had ridden and tethered them amid a clump of trees near the supply dump. Horses were much too valuable to be risked on the battlefield.

At last Alfred rose from his knees and moved forward to where his standard-bearers stood. A ripple of excitement ran through the ranks of the men. They began to shout down the hillside: "Viking scum! Prepare to die! Vengeance will be ours!"

The Vikings shouted back in the same manner. Alfred smiled to himself. This was another preparation for battle, just as important as prayers. By screaming insults and threats at their foes the men worked themselves into a frenzy of hate and determination. Alfred waited till the Saxons had reached a fever-pitch, then he raised his hand in a signal.

Trumpets blew. Immediately the shouting ceased and a wild howl arose in its place, growing louder and louder. Edwina felt her skin prickling with excitement. This, she knew, was the war-cry. The howl became a terrible shriek. The long rows of spears stabbed at the air. The line of men trembled on the brow of the ridge and then disappeared from Edwina's view as they charged

down the other side.

She *had* to see what was happening. She ran up the slope and threw herself down against a flat rock, looking over the top of it. The Saxon army was pouring down the slope beneath her. The line of men twisted out of shape on the uneven hillside. Their screaming continued as loudly as ever.

Half-way down the slope the Saxon archers dropped to their knees and drew their bows. A cloud of arrows fled hissing through the air toward the Viking ranks.

For a moment Edwina wondered if Guthrum would let his men stand there till the Saxons charged upon them, in which case they would surely be driven back at the first onslaught. But as soon as the Saxons had descended the steepest part of the slope, Guthrum raised his hand and the horn beside him blared. Then the Vikings charged, screaming their own war-cry and gaining what speed they could before the enemy weight was hurled upon them.

The lines crashed together like opposing waves in an angry sea. Spears thrust and shields rose. In an instant the orderly lines were broken into scattered fragments of fighting men grappling hand to hand. Alfred was in the midst of his men, yelling encouragement to them. Edwina could make out the dark figure of Guthrum, pointing his sword up the slope. Sigfrid was well to the front of the Viking ranks. His burly figure stood out like a human castle among the savagely fighting men and his big sword flashed in the sun as it rose and fell like a pump handle.

The sun rose high in the sky and the first furious onslaught weakened. On both sides the men drew back for breathing space. It was only a brief pause while the lines were formed afresh, a mere hundred yards apart. This time the Vikings were the first to charge, yelling frantically. The Saxon trumpet blew at once and the Saxons ran forward, still with the advantage of the downward slope. The fighting began again, as savagely as before.

Edwina wondered how long it could continue before men already tired by long marching must grow too weary to strike and defend themselves. A fear came over her that the battle might end without a victory on either side. That would surely mean yet another battle and more bloodshed. She found that she was pounding her clenched fists on the rock so hard that her skin was grazed.

Edmond, surrounded by his own party of men, was in the thick of the fighting. His arms were growing stiff from wielding his sword. He threw up his shield as a big Norseman lunged at him with a spear. The force of the blow drove the spearhead through the tough wood so that the sharp point appeared in front of Edmond's eyes. He wrenched the shield downward to break the shaft of the spear and then stabbed his sword at the man behind it. But the Norseman drew away too quickly and Edmond could no longer move the sword fast enough.

It was then that a shadow crossed his face and he looked up to see the Raven banner fluttering over his head. The line of battle had become so confused that he and his men were deep within the Viking lines. Edmond drew the last strength from his body as he darted forward. His sword rose in a sweeping arc. A scream came from the lips of the standard-bearer. He fell to the ground with Edmond on top of him. Neither was able to rise. The standard-bearer was mortally wounded while Edmond had spent his last ounce of energy. But out of the corner of his eye he could see the Raven, flat upon the ground, already being trampled into the muddy earth by the feet of struggling men.

The fall of the banner was like a signal of defeat. The Viking yells of triumph turned to cries of despair. Alfred raised a hand and the Saxon trumpet blew. His men pressed forward with all the strength they had left. Like chaff blown by a gust of wind the Vikings turned and fled toward the shelter of the wood behind them. Guthrum shouted at the top of his voice, trying to rally them, and the horn blew loudly – but all in vain.

Sigfrid was the last to turn back, still wielding his sword as if his arm as well as the weapon were made of iron.

Whooping with triumph, the Saxons chased their enemies into the wood, cutting down those they overtook.

Edwina lay against the rock at the top of the ridge, as weary as if she had taken part in the battle herself. She felt she ought to jump up and cheer. But the joy of victory faded as she stared down at the long slope beneath her. Only the dead remained there now, Vikings and Saxons huddled side by side, as if at peace with one another at last. Blood stained the ground and the scent of death already hung in the air.

Instead of cheering, Edwina wept.

LET WARS BETWEEN US CEASE

To win a kingdom for their prize
The Vikings fought, in vain.
With broken wings the Raven lies
Amid the silent slain.

GUTHRUM fled back to Chippenham with what was left of his army. He and his men took refuge within the stockade, the last bit of Wessex they could hope to defend.

Alfred halted on a hill overlooking the manor and allowed his men to rest. Next morning many of his officers wanted to attack the manor at once and complete their victory. Alfred refused.

"Guthrum still has plenty of men to defend the stockade," he declared. "To storm it would cost us many lives. Enough men have died already."

Instead, he had his army surround the manor, guarding all the roads, so that no supplies could reach the stockade.

People from the village had fled during the night, and Edwina was kept busy seeing that they were given food and shelter. Later that day two familiar figures appeared on the hillside where Alfred had set up his headquarters. Edwina ran to greet them.

"Cedric! Ellen!" she cried in relief. "Thank God you are both safe."

Alfred commanded all three of them to appear before him. He looked sternly at Edwina. "I gave you orders at Athelney that you were to take no further part in the war. It seems you disobeyed me."

Edwina bowed her head, but when she looked up again Alfred was smiling. "How can I reward you?" he said.

She had her answer ready. "Sire, before my father died he made a contract with the Thane of Mildenhall that I should marry him. I should like to be freed from this obligation."

Alfred threw back his head and laughed loudly. "Mercy, child, that wretched man was a traitor. He co-operated with the enemy. His lands shall be taken away from him and all contracts with him are cancelled. As for you being forced to marry such a fellow,

I would rather fight another battle than let it happen."

Edwina looked relieved and the king added, "I have a better idea. Let his lands be joined with those that you inherited from your father. I am sure you are well able to look after them. You will be rich, and you shall marry whom you wish. I hope that one day you will choose a husband who is worthy of you."

Alfred turned to Cedric. "For you I will create a new office. You will be the King's Poet and you will be paid a handsome salary – if you accept?"

Cedric beamed with joy as he bowed.

Then the king spoke to Ellen. "You have been a loyal servant to me as well as to Edwina. You are a servant no longer. I shall provide for you so that you may live as a lady."

Ellen's eyes widened in dismay and she shook her head. "Sire, it is not seemly that the wife of a cowherd should live like a lady. Allow me, I beg you, to serve my mistress as I have always done."

Alfred glanced at Edwina who put an arm round the little woman's shoulder. "Of course you shall if you wish," she said. "But you must promise never to lock me in the stable again."

Fourteen days after the siege began a Viking messenger left the stockade under a flag of truce. He knelt before Alfred and delivered his message, "My master, Guthrum, wishes to make peace with you. He will accept whatever terms you offer him."

It was complete surrender.

Guthrum and his senior jarls left the stockade and became hostages for the good behaviour of their men who remained at Chippenham, though Alfred treated them more like honoured guests. He took them to the Manor of Aller, which was not far from Athelney, and made them comfortable there. The two leaders, though so different in character, seemed to understand

and respect each other.

Guthrum agreed to take his army out of Wessex, and swore he would never break peace with Alfred again. But such promises had been made by Viking chiefs before, including Guthrum himself, and Alfred knew better than to put much faith in them.

One night as Alfred entertained his enemy at supper he remarked, "I know that you want to settle down with your people in a kingdom of your own. Your aim is a worthy one, though I cannot let you take my land."

Guthrum allowed himself one of his thin smiles. "I wish my men understood these things as well as you do. One day I think they will. I shall take them to East Anglia, and I shall build a new kingdom there."

Alfred nodded slowly. He felt sorry for the East Anglians, but he could not defend the whole of Britain. "If you succeed, I hope that in years to come your kingdom and mine will be at peace with one another."

"I swear by the gods—" Guthrum began, but Alfred interrupted him.

"Oaths sworn to pagan gods have little meaning. I wish that you could give me your promise as a Christian."

Guthrum looked up sharply. "Is that another condition for peace? Must I become a Christian before you will let me go?"

Alfred hesitated, choosing his words carefully. "I know I can force you if I wish, but so often in the past your chiefs have agreed to be baptised in order to make peace, and as soon as they were free they have given up Christ and returned to their old ways. I would prefer that you accept our religion with a willing heart, and persuade your men to do so too. If you really want to build a new kingdom, you will find that your people will be more loyal to their king and better able to work together if they are Christians."

The smile came faintly to Guthrum's lips once more. "I have learnt that already," he said softly.

The church at Aller was crammed with people watching the ceremony. Guthrum knelt before the font in his white christening robes. Behind him knelt Sigfrid and the other jarls, also dressed in white and looking most uncomfortable. The priest sprinkled holy water over each in turn, saying, "I baptise you in the name of the Father, of the Son and of the Holy Ghost."

When they left the church Alfred walked at Guthrum's side and they talked like old friends.

A large crowd watched them pass. Cedric was there, composing verses to suit the occasion. Edwina also stood watching with Ellen at her side. Edwina looked over the heads of the jarls and saw a young man on horseback among the thanes who formed the royal guard. He was smiling at her. He looked so clean and splendidly dressed that for a moment Edwina did not recognise him. She had never seen Edmond except in his peasant's disguise or in the sweat of march and battle.

Then she smiled back. "Doesn't he look handsome now?" she whispered to Ellen.

Ellen frowned and nudged her sharply. "Drop your eyes, child! A young lady should not exchange such bold looks with a man."

Edwina tossed her head. "We were comrades in the war," she pointed out. "Do you think I shall meet him again?"

Ellen looked at Edmond whose hand rose in greeting, and she answered with a sigh, "I have no doubt you will!"

With men and silver Guthrum paid
To free his Viking horde,
And in return one gift was made—
The blessing of the Lord.

Go hence from here to other lands,
Let wars between us cease,
And Wessex men and Viking bands
Shall learn to live in peace.

O, Christ has won the victory,
His foes have borne the loss.
Forgotten shall the Raven be,
Triumphant is the Cross.

FACT AND FICTION

Alfred became King of Wessex in 871. For nearly a hundred years Viking raiders from what is now Scandinavia had been invading the Saxon kingdoms of Britain. By Alfred's time they had overrun a good deal of northern England. They began to settle in the land and make kingdoms of their own. Wessex was much the largest Saxon kingdom still unconquered, though it had been raided many times.

Very early in January 878, when he was least expected, the Danish Chief Guthrum invaded Wessex again. He immediately captured the Royal Manor of Chippenham and then went on to overrun the major part of the kingdom. Most of the Saxon army had been disbanded for the winter and the rest were routed. Alfred was forced to take refuge among the forests and marshes which then covered a large part of Somerset.

From his hiding place Alfred organised what we would now call a "guerrilla" war against his enemies, until he was able to gather his army together again. That he was able to do this at all is proof of the strong character of the king and the loyalty which he enjoyed among the Christian Saxons. His victory over Guthrum at Edington (then Ethandun) was a turning point in the history of Britain.

After his defeat Guthrum submitted to Alfred's terms, which included Guthrum and his jarls being baptised as Christians. Then Guthrum marched his army out of Wessex and settled in East Anglia.

By the end of Alfred's reign the Norsemen and the Saxons had learnt to live in peace with one another and as a result of this the idea of an English nation arose. No wonder that the Saxon king who made it possible is remembered in history as "Alfred the Great".

All these events are historical. Other characters in this book, such as Edwina, Ellen and Cedric, are fictional and so is the story of their part in what took place – but they do provide one possible explanation of how Alfred gained such an unexpected and vital advantage over his enemies at Edington.